THE DANGER OF PROGRESSIVE LIBERALISM

THE DANGER
OF PROGRESSIVE
LIBERALISM

- - - - - - - - - - - - - - - - -

How America Is Threatened by Excessive Government,
Multiculturalism, Political Correctness, Entitlement,
and the Failures of Both Political Parties

- - - - - - - - - - - - - - - - -

Charles Gross

iUniverse, Inc.
Bloomington

The Danger of Progressive Liberalism
How America Is Threatened by Excessive Government,
Multiculturalism, Political Correctness, Entitlement,
and the Failures of Both Political Parties

iUniverse books may be ordered through booksellers or by contacting:

iUniverse
1663 Liberty Drive
Bloomington, IN 47403
www.iuniverse.com
1-800-Authors (1-800-288-4677)

Because of the dynamic nature of the Internet, any web addresses or links contained in this book may have changed since publication and may no longer be valid. The views expressed in this work are solely those of the author and do not necessarily reflect the views of the publisher, and the publisher hereby disclaims any responsibility for them.

Any people depicted in stock imagery provided by Thinkstock are models, and such images are being used for illustrative purposes only.

Certain stock imagery © Thinkstock.

ISBN: 978-1-4620-0575-8 (sc)
ISBN: 978-1-4620-0543-7 (dj)
ISBN: 978-1-4620-0542-0 (ebk)

Library of Congress Control Number: 2011904123

Printed in the United States of America

iUniverse rev. date: 04/25/2011

To Don and Virginia Gross,
Parents and Patriots

Contents

Introduction

Fueled by the aggressive actions of the progressive political Left and abetted by a political Right short on integrity, the existence of the United States of America that most of us love is in peril. Our economy is nearly bankrupt, with unsustainable national debt and out-of-control annual budget deficits. Excessive government taxation and spending overburdens our free enterprise system and enables huge groups of people to be unproductive and dependent on government programs.

Our national defense policy is not focused, we do not enforce our own immigration laws, and we have ineffective energy and environment policies. In addition, our traditional values are assaulted and the practices of multiculturalism and political correctness threaten lives and destroy the American culture.

Many voters like me, angered and threatened, have reacted by getting involved. Because of the destructive actions taken by Congress and the White House during the past several years, I determined I could no longer sit idle while watching politicians destroy our culture. I know there are many like me who will not tolerate the politics of the past, from either Democrats or Republicans. In 2010, for the first time, I actively participated in a congressional campaign, working for the candidate challenging

1

the very liberal incumbent in my district. I have increased my awareness of what happens in Washington, paying attention to how my representative and senators vote, and communicating my opinions to them. I decided to stop taking what Washington shoves down my throat and that motivation led me to write this book.

The Danger of Progressive Liberalism attempts to explain in very blunt and simple terms why we are on a disastrous path and how critical it is that we change our course. It analyzes our country's unhealthy movement to the Left since the days of Franklin Roosevelt, examines the attitude and actions of both the Left and the Right, bluntly discusses the very real threat of fundamental Islam, and offers suggestions for serious reform. Continuing the policies of the past will result in significant damage to our way of life. The solutions I offer are based on common sense and the values upon which our nation was founded. I am convinced these opinions are shared by a significant majority of the citizens of this country.

My observations are those of an average American, not a professional political pundit nor an intellectual idealist. I believe in the liberties and limited central government established by the United States Constitution and I believe most conservatives and libertarians agree. Those who consider themselves progressives or liberals may take offense at many of my statements. People often consider an opposing view as intellectually inferior, but I think one might do well to learn something about why conservatives think as they do. One might also learn something about why liberals think as they do.

I do not blame all of the problems in this country on the Left; indeed, I hold the political Right responsible for its shameful failures. When it has had the opportunity to restore the tenets of the United States Constitution and execute the will of its conservative constituency, it has failed miserably.

Our government is out of control and our country is in danger. It is the fault of both political parties and the fault of the American people for allowing what has happened in this country. We have career politicians who are so out of touch and so interested in maintaining their position that the effect is the growth of a monster called big government, a bloated entity that seems not to care about the will of the people it purports to serve. We have far too many citizens who do not hold politicians accountable. We have far too many citizens, and noncitizens, who take more from the country than they contribute.

I was fortunate, like anyone who is a citizen of the United States of America, to be given a wonderful country in which to live, work, and raise a family. I have supported this country through military service, working in private enterprise, paying taxes, following the United States Constitution, obeying the law, and being charitable and caring toward my fellow citizens. I am disgusted to witness the destruction of this great country by a coalition of progressive liberals, ignorance, complacency, greed, and irresponsible and corrupt government.

This book does not attempt to sugarcoat facts or avoid offering opinion for the sake of political correctness. I describe things as I see them. Too many people ignore facts, dodge personal responsibility, and enable bad behavior for fear of offending someone. We have created a destructive culture of political correctness and a pervasive sense of entitlement. When the government panders to that behavior, it reinforces and continues bad behavior. Far too much destructive legislation exists because the government panders to selfish and irresponsible groups, rather than executing the will of the majority.

1

What's the Problem?

Our country is on a destructive binge of governmental lunacy and personal self-absorption. We have strayed from our original principles and philosophy. We have demonized the bases on which we became the greatest country in the history of the world. We have sacrificed many of the values that formed our culture. We have often subverted or ignored the intent of the Constitution of the United States.

Our country's founders created a unique and wonderful entity, the United States of America. The very name defines our nation as an allied group of independent states, united for the common good of all. The United States was founded on the principles of a limited central government, individual liberty, self-reliance, and individual responsibility.

Over the last seventy-eight years, we have experienced a growth in government, with its attendant high costs, and a movement away from common sense. We have let the progressive liberal Left demonize and hamstring private enterprise, a basic building block of our way of life. We are becoming a nation of entitlement and disincentive. Far too many of our citizens depend on the government for much of their income. Far too much of the income taxes, paid by those who actually pay taxes, is used to support those who do not.

The power granted to the Left by a coalition of progressives, idealists, and the uninformed is extremely dangerous. The 111th Congress (January 2009–January 2011) and President Barack Obama, assisted by an irresponsibly biased media, represented a threat to American liberty and the American economy. That coalition advocated substantially bigger government, which is incompatible with American liberty. There is a very critical need to reverse that direction.

There has been a movement to the Left, socially and politically, since the 1930s. This movement has had, and is having, a destructive effect on the current and future well-being of our country. The progressive and socialist elements in our society have wielded enough influence to move political and social policy to the Left. They have basically ignored the wishes of the less organized and often passive conservatives who support traditional American values.

Progressive liberals believe the federal government should control the economy and, in many cases, the private decision-making of individuals. They continuously introduce legislation that leads to increasing the size of the federal government and spending more money. Their legislation impedes the efforts of those who would profit from free enterprise labors and intrudes more and more into decisions on how individuals conduct their lives.

Meanwhile, Republicans in Congress have been mostly incapable of doing anything beyond providing weak opposition to the Democrats' bad ideas. Rarely do Republicans demonstrate the courage and integrity necessary to return the nation to prosperity and common sense. Conservative citizens want Republicans to insist that the government live within its means, establish an environment of truly equitable opportunity and reward, and protect our country from destructive forces. Republican politicians have largely ignored the wishes of its political base, while often engaging in the same corrupt and unprincipled practices as many Democrats.

It would appear that doing what's best for the country is certainly not the first priority of many in our United States Congress. What's best for the country is a minor concern for far too many politicians, at best the fourth objective behind (1) getting elected, (2) getting re-elected, and (3) obtaining more power and wealth for themselves.

My opinion is that the majority of Americans want that which Congress is unwilling to provide. The majority of Americans do not want the size of the federal government to increase. They want it to shrink and they want to eliminate deficits. Most Americans do not want to increase taxes on any income level.

Most Americans want to protect the country, eliminate the threat of Islamic terrorism, secure our borders, and enforce our immigration laws. They want English to be the official language of the United States; they do not want to become a bilingual nation. They do not want any form of amnesty for illegal aliens.

Most Americans want to reduce dependence on foreign oil and adopt an energy policy that makes sense. They want environmental policies that are practical and efficient.

Most Americans do not want the government to run health care, do not want "Cap and Trade", do not believe in bailouts, and do not want government takeover of private enterprise.

Most Americans know health care must be reformed but do not want the government to manage it and certainly are against the unsustainable provisions of the health care bill signed into law by President Obama in 2009.

Most Americans have traditional values and do not appreciate the political correctness that protects the religious rights of others while denying the same to Christians and Jews. Most Americans want real education taught in public schools and do not approve of the heavy secular progressive liberalism taught on college campuses. They do not want multiculturalism, which is erasing the finest culture in the history of the world.

Progressive liberal politicians, as well as many Republican politicians, do not seem to listen or even care. Our federal government does not seek to execute the will of the people. Instead, it acts as though government elitists, and only them, know what's good for us. It is obvious that many in Congress believe the populace is simply too stupid to know what's best and therefore must have decisions made for them. This is particularly true of the progressive liberals on the Left, who hold the uninformed who vote for them in great contempt.

What is wrong with our elected representatives? Both sides of the aisle seem more interested in getting and keeping power than doing the right thing. Why do they renege on the promises they made which led us to vote them into office? Why do they seem to practice sleaziness and gutless vote-casting once they become immersed in the Washington culture? What is it about Washington that saps integrity and honesty and replaces it with backroom deal-making, vote-selling, and political pandering?

Part of the problem is the environment of career politicians, elected officials who become entrenched and isolated from reality. The result is their judgment becomes affected by the headiness of power, and they take the low road of ethical poverty. In later chapters, I will discuss how we might change that environment. We the people can cause the change, if only we the people make it a point to do so.

2

Definitions

We have a two-party political system: the Democrat party and the Republican party. Democrats believe in a more centralized government at the federal level, while Republicans believe in a more decentralized government. The difference is significant. The Democrat concept of democracy favors more sovereignty at the national level, whereas the Republican federal republic model favors more sovereignty at the state level. Many disagreements between the two parties are based on this distinction.

While we have only two major political parties, we have an endless array of ideologies along the political spectrum, from far Left to far Right. There are many adjectives or labels used to describe one's socio-political persuasion. So that the reader understands how I use these terms, I include definitions below. Even though some of these terms are not used in further discussion, it is useful to understand what the labels mean.

The Left, generally considered liberal, includes progressives, social liberals, social democrats, socialists, Communists, Marxists, secularists, and liberal moderates:

- Progressives: those who favor ideologies advocating changes or reform that include public (government) management and liberal social policies. Progressives align with the social liberals and social democrats and are in direct opposition to conservative and libertarian philosophies.

- Social liberals: those who believe that the state should supply individuals with the opportunity and means to support themselves. They believe that the government should intervene in the economy to provide full employment and social welfare. They typically believe in extending the rights of all citizens beyond "life, liberty, and the pursuit of happiness" to include other "rights" to basic economic advantages, such as a job, decent income, housing, and health care, among others.

- Social democrats: those who support the idea of a democratic welfare state that is both socialistic and capitalistic. Social democrats aim to reform capitalism through state regulation of the market and the creation of tax-funded welfare programs to counteract or remove the social injustices they see inherent in capitalism.

- Socialists: those who believe the means of production in an economy should be controlled by the state, rather than by individuals or capitalists. Socialists are anti-capitalists, which conservatives consider anti-American. Many modern socialists profess to be pro-capitalism, which adds ambiguity to the meaning of the term "socialist." Many on the Left bristle at being called socialist by those on the Right, because they don't want to be identified as something that is considered by most to be very anti-American.

- Communists: in the modern political sense, communism is a form of socialism, also involving an authoritarian central government that plans all aspects of the economy and controls the means of production. True communism does not allow private ownership of business and promotes the notion that everyone should be cared for by the state.

- Marxists: like socialists, Marxists advocate control of industry by the state. Marxists argue that in a capitalist society, an economic minority of capitalists exploit the working class. They believe that the working class, through political power, should have control of the means of production in collective ownership.

- Secularists: those who would remove the influence of Christianity, or any religion, from matters of state. In the pure sense, secularism requires a government to be uninfluenced by religious dogma. In today's America, secularism insists that the expression of religious dogma be repressed.

- Liberal moderates: those on the Left who are considered closer to the middle, those who do not completely align with the philosophies of the Left. Typically, they favor capitalism while also favoring some of the beliefs of social liberals. Moderates are not really true Leftists.

The Right comprises those considered to be conservatives, libertarians, reactionaries, and conservative moderates:

- Conservatives: those who support limited government interference in the free marketplace, individual ownership of capital and the means of production, prudence in government spending, a strong national defense policy, and institutions and social practices that are traditional and preserve the heritage of a nation or culture.

- Libertarians: those who support the maximization of individual liberty and the minimization of the influence of government. They believe that the central government should essentially be limited to providing an interface to other countries (State Department), national security (Defense Department), and a common currency (Treasury Department), and act as a venue to settle disputes among states of the union.

- Reactionaries: those who are extremely conservative, basically believing that society should return to an earlier, more ideal state (real or imagined). Reactionaries are quite the opposite of progressives.

- Conservative moderates: those who lean more to the Left than most other conservatives, perhaps a little to the Right of liberal moderates. They also consider themselves capitalists while agreeing with some of the beliefs of social liberals.

The term "centrist" is used to describe those who consider themselves neither Left nor Right. They may also call themselves independents. True centrists and independents do not associate with either Democrats or Republicans and may vote for a third party candidate or for the "person, not the party."

Interestingly, the Left would have you believe that Fascists, or Nazis, are also on the political Right. That is not accurate, which we'll discuss later.

3

The Progressive Movement Since FDR

From 1933, when Franklin Delano Roosevelt was first inaugurated as president of the United States, to the end of the 111th Congress in January 2011, a period of seventy-eight years, Congress was largely dominated by the Democrat party.

During those seventy-eight years, Democrats had the majority in the House of Representatives for sixty-two years, including forty consecutive years from 1955 to 1995. During those seventy-eight years, Democrats had the majority in the Senate for fifty-six years.

Republicans controlled the House for sixteen of those seventy-eight years and the Senate for twenty of those seventy-eight years. One Congress, 2001–2003, had a 50-50 deadlock in the Senate. During those seventy-eight years, Democrats controlled the House, the Senate, and the Presidency:

- For fourteen consecutive years, 1933–1947, with Franklin Roosevelt and Harry Truman

- For four consecutive years, 1949–1953, with Harry Truman

- For eight consecutive years, 1961–1969, with John Kennedy and Lyndon Johnson

- For four consecutive years, 1977–1981, with Jimmy Carter

- For two consecutive years, 1993–1995, with Bill Clinton

- For two consecutive years, 2009–2011, with Barack Obama

During the same seventy-eight years, Republicans controlled the House, the Senate, and the presidency:

- For two consecutive years, 1953–1955, with Dwight Eisenhower

- For four consecutive years, 2003–2007, with George W. Bush

So, for thirty-four of those seventy-eight years, the Democrats had majority control of the passage of legislation, while the Republicans enjoyed that advantage for only six years. For many years, the only means Republicans had available to limit Democrat control was the filibuster.

Richard Nixon, Gerald Ford, Ronald Reagan, and George H. W. Bush never had a completely friendly Congress with which to work. Eisenhower had one for only two of his eight years. George W. Bush is the only Republican president to enjoy a majority of his party in Congress for four years, or half his time in office.

Meanwhile, FDR and Truman had Democrat majorities in both sides of Congress for all but two of their combined twenty years in office. John Kennedy, Lyndon Johnson, and Jimmy Carter had Democrat majorities for their entire terms. Bill Clinton had them for his first two years in office. Barack Obama had them for his first two years.

What can be seen from these facts is that every Democrat president has had a friendly Congress for at least some of his term, while only Republicans George W. Bush and Eisenhower enjoyed the same advantage. Therefore, the Democrats have obviously enjoyed a far greater ability to advance their agenda than have the Republicans.

Considering the overwhelming dominance of the Democrat party since 1933, the inescapable conclusion is that the overall direction of the country for the past three-quarters of a century has been shaped by Democrat policy.

It is no coincidence that the size of the federal government increased dramatically during that period. While the period enjoyed a spectacular technological and industrial explosion, leading to an unprecedented standard of living, it also produced an expanding sense of entitlement and the corresponding increase in taxes necessary to support it.

Franklin Delano Roosevelt and the Democrats swept into power in 1933 with a mandate to get the country out of the Great Depression, which started with the stock market crash of 1929. Roosevelt believed the government, not private enterprise, was the vehicle to take the country on the proper course. He did not accept that private industry had the power to correct the economy if left to its own devices. He and an overwhelmingly majority Democrat Congress enacted program after program designed to cure the problem. By 1933, the national unemployment rate had reached 24.9 percent. After five years of massive government growth, the unemployment rate was still 19.0 percent.

There was a popular saying in Roosevelt's time that he did more in two weeks to try to get the country out of the Great Depression than Republican President Hoover did in the previous four years (1929–1933). There was a prevailing notion that doing a lot was better than doing little. Unfortunately, what Roosevelt did extended the depression for a decade longer than might have been the case had he done nothing but let the private sector sort it out for itself. Roosevelt's programs forever changed America from a nation of self-reliance and independence to one of considerable entitlement and dependence. Roosevelt and his liberal Democrat-dominated Congress brought the concept of the Welfare State to the American culture. This period was a tremendous shift to the Left.

In 1935, during Roosevelt's first term, the original Social Security Act was passed into law. The purpose of this legislation was to ensure the welfare of the elderly once they were no longer able to work and to provide for elderly widows. Originally, all monies collected from workers to fund Social Security were put in a trust account, so that the funds could be solely dedicated to the original purpose. That was later to change.

At the same time, the rest of the world was experiencing depression and political upheaval of its own. The result was World War II. The entry of the United States into the war focused the will of the American people, birthing a magnificent military and fueling the fantastic industrial revitalization of our economy. This economic recovery occurred *in spite of* Roosevelt's progressive policies. Interestingly, the 1930s depression was more severe in Germany than in the United States, yet Germany's recovery was much quicker, largely because Germany abstained from massive government spending programs. That also accounts for their being fully geared up for war in 1939, whereas the United States was not until 1942.

Following Roosevelt, the next eighteen years featured two moderate Democrats, Truman and Kennedy, sandwiched around the conservative Eisenhower. During this period, the conservative Right reasserted itself somewhat, taking control of the House during 1947–1949 and 1953–1955. Truman and Eisenhower both supported the independence of South Korea by taking on the Communist aggression from North Korea. Eisenhower was able to forge a peace treaty ending the Korean War in part by threatening the use of nuclear weapons against the Communists. Another of Ike's achievements was to leave office with a federal budget equal to that when he took office eight years earlier. No growth in federal government or taxes for eight years! He accomplished this by balancing the federal budget seven out of the eight years that he was president. No other modern American president has accomplished anything near this extraordinary feat.

The assassination of JFK in 1963 was a horrible tragedy. It also brought the end of fiscal responsibility by the Democrat party. One of Kennedy's achievements was introducing tax cuts for the wealthiest Americans, which helped kick off a nice run of prosperity and growth. Imagine-tax cuts for the top income earners, proposed by a Democrat president and passed by a Democrat-majority Congress!

Lyndon Johnson became president and took the country in Roosevelt's hard Left direction, with the introduction of huge government programs and increased taxes. During his administration, with the eager support of a highly liberal majority in Congress, Johnson created his group of "Great Society" programs. Those included Medicare and Medicaid, food stamps, and several environmental programs. It was Johnson's Congress that removed the provision that Social Security taxes be held in a trust fund to be used only for the intended purpose. This change put Social Security taxes into the general treasury to fund many of his programs. This is a direct cause of the imminent bankruptcy of Social Security, as conservatives tried to point out. This period was another big shift to the Left.

Following Johnson, who declined to seek another term largely because polls indicated he would not win, we had eight years of Nixon and Ford. Nixon's attempts to resolve the Vietnam conflict victoriously were doomed mostly by his political opposition, the undermining and considerably anti-American efforts of the Left. He was successful in brokering a peace treaty with North Vietnam, thus ending the war in Vietnam as a stalemate. Nixon also improved diplomatic and trade relationships with China, which opened doors to free trade globally. Unfortunately, he let his political paranoia lead him to bad decisions at home, ultimately leading to his resignation.

Gerald Ford took office after Nixon's resignation and never really had a chance to overcome the problems of his former boss. Unfortunately, during the Nixon and Ford administrations, the growth of government put in action by Johnson continued. Those two presidents were complicit, because they did not stand firm against uncontrolled growth in government. However, the major responsibility for increased federal government lies with the progressive liberal Democrat Congresses with which those presidents had to contend. Lest anyone forget, the president does not make law; Congress does.

Then we got the presidency of James Earl Carter. Viewed by many as one of the most hapless and incompetent presidents ever, the policies of Jimmy Carter and his liberal Democrat Congress brought us unprecedented inflation and unemployment, decimation of our military prowess, and international embarrassment. One of his economic disasters was extending Social Security annuity payments to immigrants, whether they had paid into the system or not. Carter's time, thankfully only one term, gave us another shift to the Left.

What followed Carter was one of the greatest resurgences our nation has ever enjoyed. When Ronald Reagan swept Carter out of office, he ushered in an era of restored American pride and leadership. Like him or not, history credits Reagan with ending the cold war without firing a shot. This victory ended an intense struggle for control of the world and the threat of nuclear annihilation. There has never been an equivalent accomplishment by any other world leader. Reagan also restored the nation's sense of self-reliance and optimism that had withered in the previous years.

Reagan's popularity helped his vice president, George H. W. Bush, win the White House in 1989. President Bush was boxed in by a hostile Congress and thus not able to maintain his predecessor's momentum. His attempt at a second term was torpedoed by the insistence of Ross Perot to run as a third party candidate. Perot took nearly 20 percent of the vote in the 1992 election, most of which would have been votes for Bush. Perot's insistence on being heard cost conservatives a presidential election and illustrates how a three political party system can lead to an unpopular selection.

So, in 1992, the country elected William Jefferson Clinton as president even though he gained only 43 percent of the popular vote. Four years later, Clinton won re-election with 49 percent of the popular vote. He is the only president to serve two terms without ever getting the majority of the vote.

Bill Clinton's presidency was remarkable for many reasons. One was his persistent practice of governing according to polls. Almost every decision he made was heavily influenced by how it would affect his popularity. His lack of reaction to multiple terrorist activities against the United States demonstrated his desire not to upset any apple carts or alarm any factions. Apparently, his governing style was to avoid doing anything that might make him unpopular.

Clinton came into office with the idea of promoting several Leftist programs. The health care reform that he favored was met with decisive opposition. However, early in his presidency he managed to increase the size of the federal government and get legislation passed to tax Social Security benefits. Keep in mind that in earlier years, Democrats had changed the original Social Security legislation so that money deducted from paychecks for Social Security had already been subject to income tax. Now, with Al Gore casting the deciding vote in the Senate (the vote was 50-50), recipients of Social Security benefits must pay income taxes on those benefits. This was another shift to the Left.

During Clinton's second term, the Newt Gingrich-led Republican resurgence and takeover of the majority in the House kept Clinton in check during the rest of his presidency, a fact quite overlooked when people assess Clinton's effectiveness. Liberals like to point to Clinton as a model of fiscal leadership; they either miss the real story or ignore the facts.

Then we elected George W. Bush. Early in his administration, with an agreeable Congress, he was able to reverse the recession he inherited (the market had peaked in March 2000 and was headed south when Bush took office in January 2001). The Bush tax cuts, a reduction in taxes for all wage earners, helped fuel a nice run of growth and prosperity. Unfortunately, Bush and the Republican majority failed to control spending and rein in disastrous Democrat programs.

The Democrats took back control of both the House and the Senate in January 2007 and absolutely refused to work with Bush to stop the impending banking and housing collapse. Bush sponsored legislation to reverse irresponsible lending practices enacted during the Clinton years that provided government-backed home loans for people who could not afford them. He also sponsored legislation to reverse the continued growth of federal employment. However, a Congress that at best was in denial, at worst corrupt and dishonest, defeated those proposals. Bush warned us and asked Congress to do something to prevent disaster, but the people didn't listen and Congress wouldn't do it.

In what appears to be one of history's most sinister actions by our country's leadership, the Democrat Congress of 2007–2009 sat back and let the economic disaster occur, when they had the means to stop it. They relied on ignorance on the part of the public, which would let them blame it on the Republican administration. Thus they could ride the outrage over the collapse to victory in November 2008. In the summer of 2008, McCain/Palin had edged ahead of Obama/Biden in the polls but lost that lead when the economy tanked a couple of months prior to the election. Was it an engineered crisis?

That brings us to the 111th Congress of 2009–2011 and the presidency of Barack Hussein Obama. During his first two years, there were dozens of new taxes imposed, and the government took control of huge segments of the private sector. The federal government took over the banking industry, the college loan industry, a large part of the domestic automobile industry, the health care industry, and more. The encroachment of the federal government into private life escalated enormously. This two-year period was a swift and enormous shift to the Left.

We now have about half of the population paying less into the government than they are taking. Close to 40 percent of the country pays no taxes at all, and another large number pay much less taxes than the benefits they receive. The federal deficit has skyrocketed since Obama took office in January 2009. The annual federal budget deficit under George Bush, so assaulted by the progressive Left and the liberal media, has more than tripled under Barack Obama.

The rising budget deficits cause a parabolic increase in the total national debt. In other words, the amount of our total national debt is increasing at a faster and faster rate. It reminds me of the stuck accelerator problem that causes automobiles to go faster and faster, out of control. Without corrective action, at some point a tremendous crash is inevitable.

The notion that it is necessary to spend money to get out of debt, as postulated by the progressive liberals of the Left, is so ludicrous that only someone completely deluded or devoid of logic would buy it. Similar to the mistakes of the 1930s, the economy is hindered by the continuing efforts of the government to fix it. At least with Roosevelt's massive spending, the country got a few tangible things out of it, such as the Hoover Dam.

The current administration and the liberal media continue to insist that the current economic woes are the fault of the previous administration. Remember, the progressive liberal Democrats took control of Congress in 2007, two years before the end of the Bush administration. So, after four years of Democrat control in Congress and two years of the leadership of the Barack Obama administration, we are in far worse economic shape, yet the far Left and the administration still claim it's the fault of George Bush.

4

What the Left Thinks

The Left includes people with a diverse array of personalities, income levels, intellectual abilities, educational achievements, patriotism, and general knowledge. Most who describe themselves as liberal or progressive vote for Democrat political candidates. There are also many moderates and some conservatives who vote Democrat but do not share the values of the progressive Left. By the same token, not all Republicans are truly conservative.

Sometimes, politicians associate themselves with the party that gives them the best chance of election, regardless of philosophical alignment. Some districts are very liberal and unlikely to elect a Republican. Some districts are very conservative and unlikely to elect a Democrat. Therefore, to increase the chances of being elected, a fairly conservative candidate may run as a Democrat, or a fairly liberal one may run as a Republican.

My argument is not Democrat versus Republican. By no means do I consider all Democrats bad and all Republicans good. From a conservative's point of view, there are many reasonable

Democrats, and there certainly are some really rotten Republicans. My focus is progressive liberalism versus conservatism.

It is difficult for conservatives to understand how an American could think the way progressive liberals do. We don't understand how someone could consider him- or herself patriotic and be supportive of progressive liberal causes that assault the United States Constitution, the American private enterprise system, and traditional American liberty and morality.

Conservatives and libertarians can generally be counted on to share certain values. That is not as true of liberals. The Left comprises a broad range of political opinions and positions. There is a very significant difference between those who are hard Left secular progressives and those who are moderate liberals.

Supporters of the Democrat party, which promotes the progressive Leftist agenda, include the rich and the poor, the intelligent and the unintelligent, the educated and the profoundly ignorant, scholars and dropouts, patriots and bashers of America, hard workers and the entitlement class. The following groups of people include many who support progressivism and vote Democrat:

- Academia

- Entertainers

- The media

- The profoundly uninformed

- The poor

- Labor unions

- Young adults

- Trial lawyers and judges

It should go without saying this is a generalization; certainly not everyone in these groups is a progressive liberal. However, a significant majority of them are.

* * * * *

There are quite a few people whose values are not those of progressive liberals but, for whatever reason, continue to vote with the Democrats and may even describe themselves as liberals. These are voters who are actually opposed to much of what liberals promote, who believe in basic conservative values but still elect progressive liberal politicians, essentially believing one way and voting another. These are people who conduct their lives like conservatives, yet prefer to call themselves Democrats. Apparently, they believe that the ideals of the Left are nobler, fairer, less selfish, and more inclusive, not acknowledging the assault on their values by the Left.

The Democrat party continues to move steadily toward the Left, dragging the entire political system with it. Many moderate Democrats have been replaced with more progressive ones, and the very liberal among them have become more powerful. This has left behind the remaining moderate "Blue Dog" Democrats.

The move to the Left has caused many moderate or conservative Democrat voters to change their allegiance. Traditional southern Democrats are good examples. For generations, all Deep South states could be counted on as sure things by Democrat politicians. That began to change as this group realized where the progressives like Lyndon Johnson and Jimmy Carter (ironically from Texas and Georgia, respectively) were taking the country. They began to see they had little in common with the secular progressives far to their Left. Since Carter's time, the Deep South has become conservative Republican territory.

However, there are many who are moderate or conservative who apparently believe the Democrat party is still what it once may have been. Harry Truman and John Kennedy were Democrats who believed in fiscal responsibility, a strong national defense, and traditional American values. They are vastly different from most contemporary Democrats, who are far more liberal. Perhaps many moderates who support today's Democrats inherited the voting tendencies of their parents and do not recognize or consider how times and their party have changed They are possibly also motivated by an inherited distrust of anything associated with Republicans.

* * * * *

Many intellectuals consider themselves liberals and support the progressivism of the Left. These intellectuals believe in idealism and typically don't acknowledge when those ideals don't work in the real world. Persons with the highest IQs are not always the most informed and practical people. The average IQ of small business owners or managers in large companies is undoubtedly lower than the average college professor. Many intellectuals learn at the altar of liberal teaching in our schools and have a tendency to closet themselves within their area of intellectualism. They limit their associations to others much like themselves and can be quite detached from the mainstream citizenry.

Many intellectuals value wit and cleverness over mundane common sense. They value eloquence more than down-to-earth straight talk. Intellectuals are much more likely to consider intellectualism and eloquence as prerequisites for leadership. However, history is full of examples that contradict such thinking.

Many of history's greatest leaders were certainly not the most intellectual persons of their times. Great leaders make great decisions. Idealists and intellectuals often are not great leaders. Intellectualism does not imply wisdom. In fact, my opinion is that many intellectuals on college campuses are quite ignorant of practical matters and common sense.

Liberal intellectuals ridiculed the oratory abilities of George Bush. Progressive liberals and socialists in other countries lambasted his speaking skills, apparently causing much embarrassment to American liberals. The same intellectuals expressed their great satisfaction with the eloquence and oratory manner of Barack Obama, treating his charismatic speaking as though it were indicative of greater leadership ability.

Consider the eloquent, emotional, and charismatic leaders of the past century. For every John Kennedy, Martin Luther King, Jr., or Ronald Reagan, there has been a Vladimir Lenin, Adolph Hitler, or Fidel Castro.

The quality of our government-run public elementary, middle, and high schools is seriously declining, largely because of the influence of teachers' unions. However, we in the United States enjoy the best post-high school educational opportunities and have the greatest access to the best learning centers in the world. The very bright often favor opportunities in education, research, journalism, and other areas outside the world of business and industry. Many intellectuals choose career environments that foster idealism, such as classrooms, research labs, law, journalism, or other areas that are not part of the mainstream capitalist environment.

The pervading attitude on college campuses is extremely progressively liberal. As far back as more than a century ago, many American universities became havens for transplanted

European intellectuals. They brought their European model of human rights, which tended to be along the Left spectrum, from progressive liberalism to socialism and Marxism. Over time, their progressive thinking supplanted on our college campuses the traditional American values of common sense and self-reliance.

The influence of progressives and socialists on American campuses has been on a steady increase for quite some time, at least since the early twentieth century. The college campus offers sanctuary and support to thinking that would meet considerable opposition in the working world. As more Leftist thought gets nurtured on the campus, more Leftist ideas take hold among students, fostering an environment that is increasingly friendly to the Left and oppressive to the Right. The learning environment on college campuses today is clearly heavily Leftist. Obviously, the more time in that environment, the more likely one will adopt Leftist idealisms.

Many American universities have faculties in their liberal arts colleges that do not include a single member who would describe him- or herself as a conservative. Not a single one! The reason is that the state board of regents does not hire professors, nor does the university president. Hiring of new faculty is done by the existing faculty. A conservative has virtually no chance of being hired by the highly progressive liberal faculties in many liberal arts colleges. That explains much of the extreme bias that exists in the teaching on American campuses.

Many liberal intellectuals have a low view of the capacity of the average citizen to be moral and just. They have little tolerance for those who do not think as they do. The intellectual liberal mind believes it must determine what is fair and best for everyone else. It cannot accept the notion that lesser brains can take care of themselves. They believe that the average person is likely to be racist, greedy, homophobic, sexist, and unfair. They support the intervention of the central government to control that behavior and implement their ideal of government-mandated equality rather than individual liberty.

The irony is that the caring words of progressive liberals do not translate to their attitudes and actions. They tout the ideal of equality for everyone while harboring their arrogant disdain for others.

It was a very impressive group of intellectuals, some not particularly educated, who framed the United States Constitution. It is a far less impressive group of modern intellectuals who think nothing of ignoring or challenging the Constitution, as it suits their secular, progressive, liberal views. I'm sure they view themselves as intellectually superior to those "old men" in the eighteenth century.

More college education does not translate to a better appreciation of our country's founding principles or of patriotism. Apparently, the higher the college degree, the less likely one is to consider the United States a force for good in the world community, but rather that the United States corrupts otherwise good people. That is much more likely true among those in the arts than those in business and science.

The brightest students are also less likely to have worked in the private sector throughout college and certainly less likely to have served in the armed forces of the United States. Generally, people without private sector or military experience are more likely to lean to the Left politically. We saw in the 1960s and 1970s the emergence of heavy anti-American, anti-military, anti-establishment sentiment in academia. No wonder that the drug-using, war-protesting, free love flower children of that time influenced many liberals a generation later.

When discussing the concept of multiculturalism in Western societies, esteemed columnist Thomas Sowell noted that the problems associated with welcoming foreign workers who chose to remain foreign are so obvious that only the intelligentsia could fail to see them. A profound line he used in that discussion was "It takes a high IQ to evade the obvious." Too often, that's the case.

* * * * *

Consider those in the entertainment world. Why are so many performing artists and television personalities so far Left? Certainly most of them are neither profoundly unintelligent nor extremely intellectual, and certainly most of them actually work for a living and are rewarded for the work they do.

Celebrities are detached from the rest of society and have little in common with, or understanding of, those who work in business and industry. They can be incredibly self-absorbed and insulated from reality. The modern Hollywood, television, or music idol is not likely to have much education or experience in areas like business, economics, finance, or science, and they almost certainly did not serve in the United States armed forces. Like university professors and scholastic intellectuals, movie and television personalities tend to associate with others like themselves and do not really understand, empathize with, or relate to those in the mainstream. There is almost nothing that would qualify most entertainers to have any meaningful judgment about anything outside their realm of artistic expertise.

Unfortunately, entertainment personalities have a great big soapbox available to them. It is amazing that so many people will ingest the vigorous pontifications of a modestly educated and heavily biased personality, someone with little education in or experience with the subjects about which they have such convicted opinions. Remember the roster of entertainers who loved to call George Bush stupid? President Bush earned a bachelor's degree from Yale and a master's degree from Harvard. He is the only president to ever have earned the degree of master of business administration. One particular singer/actress who called Bush's intelligence into question did not herself graduate from high school. I find that laughable and pathetic.

Many celebrities engage in charitable causes and have a sincere desire for improving the lives of others. Perhaps there is something in the type of personality that gravitates toward the performing arts that also includes a good dose of humanity. However, that doesn't equate to an understanding of economics, foreign policy, national defense, or many other major concerns of society.

Entertainment celebrities often demonstrate a troubling "above the law" attitude. Have you ever noticed how celebrities will excuse outrageous behavior among their own? The outrageous behavior could be treasonous, sexually deviant, or abusive—it doesn't matter. The progressive Left is far more willing to ignore and even defend behaviors that mainstream citizens consider very wrong, thus it makes sense for those celebrities to take safe harbor among their liberal friends.

Fewer and fewer movies promote traditional patriotic American values. Hollywood portrays America as belligerent and war-mongering because that plays well on foreign screens. So does portraying American capitalism as sinister and greedy. Hollywood will happily produce a film that reinforces negativity toward America for the profits America-bashing generates from abroad. The hypocrisy is interesting—making money through American capitalism by bashing American capitalism.

Have you ever thought about how Hollywood was founded? Entrepreneurs, seeking fame and fortune from the appetite of the public for the new entertainment technology, founded the motion picture studios. Without the capitalistic energy and risk-taking, even greed, of those founders, perhaps there would be no platform for today's celebrities to denounce such behavior.

* * * * *

Perhaps the type of personality that aspires to a career in the news media is similar to that of celebrities, but without the acting or singing talent.

The majority of those in the news media tend to have a similar disassociation with the rest of us and live in a world where sensationalism and alarmism are rewarded. They seem to try to one-up each other in their zeal to praise or criticize that which has their attention. If the subject is attractive to them, the foaming at the mouth is ridiculous. If the subject is objectionable, the vitriol goes beyond any sense of fairness or reason. For an obvious reference, consider the liberal media's treatment of two important political candidates in 2008 (and beyond)—the Democrat presidential candidate and the Republican vice presidential candidate.

That's an interesting aside, by the way. The liberal media pulled off one of the biggest shell games of all time, which was playing Obama against Bush, who wasn't on the ballot, and Palin, the Republican nominee for the number two spot. John McCain was a war hero, admired and respected by most Americans, so the media avoided excessive criticism of him. They understood how mean that would appear. Not so for Bush and Palin. At the same time, they basically just gave Biden a media pass. Thus, the campaign became Hope and Change (never mind the ridiculous vagueness of that concept) against the perceived failures of Bush and the alleged lack of experience of Palin.

The liberal media lambasted Palin's experience: four years on a small town city council, six years as its mayor, two years as Alaska's governor, and several years experience as a small business owner (apparently worthless to a capitalism hater). At the same time, they slobbered over a candidate whose credentials consisted of working as a community organizer, a civil rights attorney, a law professor, about six years as a state senator, less than one full term in the United States Senate, and zero experience in the private sector.

Governor Palin was also the commander-in-chief of the only state National Guard that is continuously on active duty because of its proximity to Russia. Senator Obama had no armed forces experience whatsoever.

Never mind that Palin's career was one of consistent success. The media was able to convince enough moderate voters to believe the potential horror of Palin being one (McCain) heartbeat away from the presidency, while ignoring the actual horror of the vastly inexperienced Obama.

The bias of the mainstream media is obvious and pervasive. If the majority of Americans did not get their (mis)information from those media, the Democrat party could not advance its current hard Left agenda. Unfortunately, enough of the population is influenced by the media bias, completely ignoring facts and logic, to put power in the hands of the extreme Left.

If you pay attention to what many entertainment and media personalities have to say, you should notice a double standard. A Republican is blasted as a racist for making the same type of thoughtless remark as a Democrat, but the Democrat's remark is ignored, or lamely explained. A-List actors and the mainstream media ripped Bush for his supposed lack of response to Katrina in 2005 but hardly mentioned the shameful lack of leadership of the governor of Louisiana and the mayor of New Orleans.

Did those enlightened entertainers and media people bother to understand or consider the legal succession of responsibility in such situations? Original responsibility for responding to local disasters belongs to local government, which must officially request assistance from its state government. If necessary, the state government must officially request assistance from the federal government. The federal government is prohibited from intervening without the official request.

The same Bush-haters had little negative to say about the indecisive response of President Obama to the Gulf oil spill in 2010. They said nothing about his lack of response to the devastating flooding in other parts of the country. At least Obama was somewhat nonpartisan in his lack of concern. He ignored the devastating floods and tornadoes in the conservative South and Midwest and the devastating floods in the more liberal New England.

The progressive liberals called Bush and Cheney racists, though they appointed more minorities to leadership positions in government than any previous administration and were never guilty of racist comments. The same unprofessional, irresponsible media liberals do not report on the slew of racist remarks made by Democrats, particularly minority Democrats.

Most interestingly, the very well paid entertainment and media personalities blast the hand that has richly fed them (business) while lavishly enjoying the meal. The top Hollywood stars are very wealthy businesspersons, enjoying the financial rewards their talent brings them, yet somehow they rationalize condemning our capitalistic system for its greed and corruption. Did I mention hypocrisy earlier?

Of course there are celebrities and media personalities who are not progressive liberals. We hear less from them than the liberals for the obvious reason that most in the media are also liberals.

* * * * *

A significant number of citizens who side with the Left are people who don't think much at all. A distressingly large percentage of the population is shockingly ignorant. You've seen them interviewed humorously by talk show hosts, exit poll takers, and others. These are the people who can't answer very basic questions about subjects that should be considered simple common knowledge.

I read a report recently about questions posed to high school graduates that revealed an astounding lack of knowledge. "Who was our nation's first president?" was correctly answered by fewer than half of high school seniors. The great majority could not identify the current Speaker of the House, the Senate majority leader, or the vice president. Only one in five knew the number of United States senators or that each state has two. Many citizens, even many with a high school diploma and perhaps a college degree, are astonishingly ignorant, knowing almost nothing about geography, history, math, science, economics, literature, civics, and certainly not the causes and effects of public policy.

An exit poll of voters taken just after they made their selections for president, congressperson, senator, other local offices, and various amendments, on Election Day 2008, demonstrated a stunning ignorance. In one heavily Democrat precinct, most voters could not answer extremely simple and basic questions about the people for whom they had voted. Almost no one polled could speak with any knowledge whatsoever about the voting records of the two presidential candidates.

The great majority of those who are this uninformed generally support Democrats. Here is why:

- There is a perception that Democrats care more and do more to help the underprivileged, poorly educated, and impoverished.

- It is far easier for the uninformed and uneducated to understand a promise of help through welfare and other handouts (the liberal Democrat position) than to understand the complexities of how the free enterprise system provides more opportunity and ultimately less poverty (the conservative position).

- Democrat politicians understand this and pander to the uninformed with promises, often deceptive and utterly unrealistic.

- The uninformed, regardless of economic status, rely more on eloquence and emotional appeal in determining for whom to vote.

- Republicans don't appeal as well to the ignorant. Positions like advocating lower taxes for everyone is perceived (and played by liberals and the liberal media) as favoring the wealthy. Many uninformed are influenced by the Left's constant portrayal of Republicans as rich, greedy people who care nothing for others.

- Standard Republican ideals, such as insisting on following the Constitution, don't mean as much to people who don't even know what the Constitution says.

- The chronically unemployed, as well as the poor and the uninformed, look for government intervention, and it is most often offered, or at least perceived to be offered, by Democrats.

- There is a sadly growing attitude of entitlement and lack of self-reliance in our country that is cultivated and enabled by liberal Democrat policies.

Many who are profoundly uninformed do not vote at all. Most conservatives are relieved they don't, because of the tendency of the ignorant to vote with the liberals. It is not merely a caring civic gesture for so many Democrats to work to get out the vote of those who otherwise wouldn't bother. It is in their interests. My guess is that there are a great number of people who are considerably uninformed, perhaps as much as half the population. That's a lot of potential votes.

* * * * *

Much like the NAACP, large American labor unions no longer provide positive solutions to unfairness in society or in the workplace. Union bosses are now unapologetic plunderers of the companies for which they work and of the American taxpayer. It is obvious that the overarching concerns of big labor are "How can I work fewer hours?", "How much time off can I have?", "How much health insurance can I get?", "How can I assure myself that I'll get paid, even when my employer is losing money or I'm on furlough?", "How can I get promoted, regardless of my qualifications?", "How can I be assured I won't be disciplined or lose my job, even when I've been unproductive or incompetent?", and "How early can I retire and how big will my pension be?" Big labor union contracts almost guarantee higher costs for lower performance.

All that certainly sounds like the entitlement attitude of those other groups who believe in rewards for nothing. Which political party makes the most promises to big labor? Which political party gets the vast majority of contributions from big labor? Which political party panders to the "poor, oppressed worker" who is purportedly somehow exploited by greedy corporate management? Of course the answer is the Democrat party.

* * * * *

There is an old saying: "If you aren't a liberal when you're twenty, you don't have a heart, but if you aren't a conservative when you're forty, you don't have a brain." This quip is not as facetious as it might seem. Youthful idealism and relative inexperience combine to make liberalism seem more humane and fair. Progressive liberalism appeals to emotion and idealism, not necessarily to logic and practicality.

Conservatism promotes personal responsibility, providing for oneself, not looking to the government for help, and assisting others to do likewise. Conservatives admire experience, traditional values, and prudence, in an environment of limited government interference. Young adults don't have a lot of experience, tend to challenge tradition and create new values, and tend to be somewhat rash. The notion of government interference might not be particularly negative to this group. Most of us agree that children who don't have to work and pay for anything do not learn the value of money. Until someone works and pays taxes, there is not as much reason to care much about government fiscal responsibility. Until one's liberties are oppressed, the existence of big government might not be so threatening.

The young are more likely influenced by those in the entertainment world. The nonsense of that group, along with liberal teaching in schools, creates a tendency for the young to identify with the Left. That is, until many of them grow up, get a job, pay taxes, and worry about their children's future.

* * * * *

Many trial lawyers stand to benefit from progressive liberals' support of divisiveness and victimhood. Obviously lawyers make a lot of money from the lawsuits of victims. The most sensational ones usually pit a poor victim against a corporation described as uncaring or criminal. Malpractice cases against doctors profit lawyers while driving up the costs for doctors to do business. Republicans favor tort reform legislation, which would reduce these costs, yet Democrats disagree.

Lawyers invented and maintain a foreign language that ordinary people have difficulty understanding. It is called legalese, and one of its principal reasons for being is to ensure the necessity of lawyers who can read and speak it. Consider the massive United States Tax Code. That set of documents by itself is enough to keep thousands of lawyers busy making tons of money.

Once they have had enough practicing law and want to take on something new, the two obvious career paths for attorneys are politics or judgeships. The number of senators and representatives who hold law degrees or formerly practiced law is usually more than one third. Of course, almost all judges are lawyers.

At the federal level, those classified as Article III judges are appointed for life by the president and confirmed by the Senate. That includes Justices of the Supreme Court, appeals court judges (also called circuit court judges), and United States district court judges, a total of around 3,500 judges. They can be as capricious and illogical as they want, and the worst that may happen is that their decisions get overturned by a higher court, up to the Supreme Court. In an extreme case, they may be removed, but that requires impeachment by the United States House of Representatives and conviction by the United States Senate. In addition, Congress may not reduce an Article III federal judge's salary unless he or she is removed through the expensive and time-consuming impeachment/conviction process. A judge could be behind bars for a crime and still drawing full salary before Congress becomes motivated to pursue removal.

Far too many federal judges apply a liberal bias to their interpretation of the Constitution, quite often in defiance of the will of the great majority of the people. Of course there are many lawyers and judges who are not progressive liberals and who do not support Democrat policy. I know a few, including my ex-brother-in-law, who was a fine criminal attorney and who is a fine, patriotic, conservative American.

* * * * *

I believe the single core value among these groups on the Left is the harboring of an extreme disdain for conservative thinking and Republicans in general. They insist that Republicans include and represent the well-off at the expense of the less fortunate. They consider those on the Right to be greedy and uncaring about the plight of those who are less privileged. The substantial majority of business owners and others successful in private enterprise are conservatives and vote Republican. Therefore, liberals consider their hypothesis proven, whether or not it's at all accurate.

Liberals do a lot of wishful thinking. Much of their thinking is based on how things ought to be in a just and fair world, regardless of common sense, practicality, or logic. This thinking is shared by both the very intelligent and the very ignorant.

Liberals have the eager and professionally irresponsible bias of much of the mainstream media to support their often misguided and destructive policies. With such support, the progressive Left is able to wreak havoc on the country and convince a lot of people that the blame lies with the Republicans.

Another perception harbored by the Left is race and gender based. Many liberals typecast conservatives as white and predominantly male. Democrats have had a lot of success in painting Republicans and conservatives as being less supportive of the rights of women and racial minorities. The Democrat party claims to be the one that cares about women's rights, including abortion. The Democrat party claims to be the one that supports the struggles of racial minorities. That those claims are not altogether accurate does not matter to most liberals.

Liberals consider themselves the only people who care about such issues as global warming/climate change, the environment, and energy. Liberals associate big business with environmental destruction and reckless mistreatment of animal life, human life, and life in general. Liberals are alarmists: "The polar ice cap is melting!" "Corporate American is killing people!" "The Canadian fox has no place to live!" "People are starving!" Professional liberals are very adept at pointing the blame for any reckless mistreatment of our planet and its inhabitants on corporate America and Republicans. Of course, the fact that American corporations and conservatives are actually more environmentally conscious than the average liberal does not matter or does not register with a liberal.

Liberals do not credit American business for its efforts to operate with environmental care. Liberals generally dislike and distrust capitalism. Conservatives value capitalism. Whereas conservatives view capitalism as a force for good, providing jobs and increasing the standard of living for all, liberals view capitalism as an evil that seeks to reward the greedy at the expense of the less fortunate. Never mind that most liberals have no problem enjoying the benefits of the endeavors of private enterprise.

Notice a common thread among the groups on the Left that I listed above: the absence of private enterprise involvement. Most liberals disdain the greedy notion of profits, identifying capitalists with selfishness. Even labor unions, who profit greatly when their employers are successful, act in opposition to "greedy" management, while maintaining their pervasive sense of entitlement.

Liberals are less likely to be supportive of and participate in the national defense efforts of our United States military. In the face of conflict or threat, liberals are more likely to favor appeasement than more aggressive alternatives. It is interesting to see liberals wear flag pins and espouse support for our troops while supporting measures that undermine the mission of those troops.

Liberals do not value adherence to the United States Constitution and Bill of Rights as rigorously as do conservatives. I believe many of them consider those documents as somewhat appropriate for the times in which they were written and as useful in helping us gain our independence, but archaic now. After all, it was a bunch of white males who wrote those documents, and many of them were chauvinists and slave-owners, they would say. Liberals often think nothing of changing or ignoring the Constitution, as it suits their purposes.

Liberals value the concept of equality as opposed to equal opportunity. They believe that removing barriers to opportunity is not enough to help those who need help the most. They think that simply opening all doors to everyone will result in only the privileged being able to walk through those doors. Many further believe that everyone should enjoy more or less equal success, equal material goods, and equal access to comforts and even luxuries. Since this can only be accomplished by providing more assistance to those deemed "less equal," they believe that the role of the government is to make it so. Democrat politicians are only too happy to appear to accommodate that belief.

Liberals believe in a more active and robust role of the federal government in practically all areas of life. Rather than depend upon and trust the private sector, they value the role of the government in making everything fair for everyone. Frankly, I really don't think a lot of liberals are so interested in making things fair. Many of them are interested in making things better only for the groups they identify as deserving of special treatment, often meaning themselves. Their view of personal rights usually means their rights, not necessarily those of others. As the brilliant, intellectual conservative Ann Coulter points out, "Liberals have two sets of rules: one for themselves and one for everyone else."

Further, liberals expect more in the way of support and benefits from external sources, rather than depending on self-reliance. This reflects itself in several ways: demands on employers, insistence on government intervention and support, demands for public assistance, and off-loading personal responsibility onto others or onto circumstances they cannot control.

Liberals view conservatives as staid, greedy, racist, sexist, homophobic, and morally and intellectually inferior. Try as you might, it is difficult to convince a convicted liberal otherwise. You can be warm and friendly, work hard and pay taxes, raise a decent family, believe in equal opportunity and liberty for all, treat everyone with respect, be generous to charities, act frugally, conserve energy, do volunteer work, leave the handicapped spots for those who need them, have gay and minority friends, and recycle your cans, plastic, papers, and bottles. However, to a liberal you are morally and intellectually inferior if you vote Republican or call yourself a conservative or libertarian.

Liberals cannot acknowledge the notion that a conservative might be intelligent, compassionate, and reasonable. Liberals cannot accept any view other than their own. The only way liberals can rationalize conservative outrage at progressive policy is to attach one or more of their standard divisive and hate-filled labels to conservatives. When logic and facts are not available to support the liberal argument, as is often the case, the fallback is to play the race card, the Nazi card, the homophobia card, the greedy card, or any other card in the deck.

I remember once, when a liberal female became frustrated in a political discussion with me, she ended the conversation with

"Oh, just go play your racist, chauvinist, elitist, Republican game of golf." I think she demonstrated how a lot of liberals think.

Another standard liberal rebuttal when presented with facts is "Well, you have your opinion and I have mine." Sometimes, when facts are facts, there is no opinion. Liberals do not recognize the logic of that. A conservative might argue a point of difference by presenting a statistic only to have the position dismissed as opinion. Here's a discussion typical of many I've had with a liberal, starting with my statement:

"Obama promised to keep unemployment from rising above 8 percent, yet it rose from 8 to 10 percent in his first fifteen months."

"That's Bush's fault."

"But Obama's stimulus package, designed to reverse the increase in unemployment, was passed by the Democrat-controlled Congress and signed by Obama in February 2009, when Bush was no longer in office."

"Obama inherited the bad economy from Bush."

"Maybe you didn't understand me. Obama promised the stimulus package would provide more jobs, but it didn't. That was after Bush."

"That's just your opinion."

End of discussion.

5

What the Left Says

The Left portrays itself as the champion of many seemingly righteous social and political causes. Many on the Left sincerely believe they are the guardians of the rights and welfare of those who would otherwise be trampled by the more advantaged in our society. Leftist politicians claim to be the friend and protector of the disadvantaged, the environment, so-called minorities, laborers, and, in general, anyone and anything that is a "victim." With considerable help from Hollywood, the liberal media, unions, and educators, the Left is able to sell this notion.

Unfortunately, many progressive liberals do not understand or consider the consequences of Leftist policy. They do not concern themselves with the actual impact of government intervention, higher taxes, weak national defense policy, so-called multiculturalism, and political correctness.

As mentioned earlier, practically all conservatives favor smaller government, lower taxes, strong national defense, and traditional family values. The policy of progressive liberals promotes just the opposite: bigger government, higher taxes, weaker national defense, and destruction of family values.

However, Democrats cannot run for office saying they want to increase taxes and the size of the government, weaken the military, and change American values, because the majority of people don't want that. Perhaps when Obama started using language like "fundamentally transform America," voters should have swooned a bit less and looked into what he meant by fundamental transformation.

Liberal Democrat politicians talk about providing programs to care for people but fail to mention that the result is bigger government. They talk about raising taxes on the wealthy, on corporations, on large inheritances, on anything other than the middle and lower class. They don't talk about the result being more taxes on everyone, including the middle and lower income workers. They talk about controlling military spending but don't mention how their idea of controlling means reducing our military capability. They talk about tolerance, diversity, and multiculturalism but don't mention the negative effect on the morality and values of our young people.

In many cases, a liberal politician will avoid campaigning on the issues of national defense or the economy. This was especially true in the 2010 campaign season, when so many voters had become so decidedly against the direction Democrats had taken the country. The economy worsened in the first two years of Obama's presidency, and many people quit buying the idea that it was someone else's fault, that the Leftist Obama/Pelosi/Reid agenda was not to blame. Therefore, Democrat politicians who had supported that agenda were in a bind. Many of them tried to distance themselves from Obama/Pelosi/Reid, in some cases pretending they did not really support that which they had voted for. Others found it best to try to steer the discussion away from the big issues, like the economy, and talk about wedge issues, like racism and gay rights.

The latter allows a liberal to change the discourse to their old standard tactic of identifying groups of people as victims. If there is a victim, it is necessary to have a villain, which the Left is quick to identify as the political Right. If you examine the rhetoric of the Left, you will see how they continuously advance the idea of victim and villain, insisting that certain groups are taken advantage of or discriminated against. This mentality creates and maintains emotional causes that liberal Democrat politicians are only too happy to exploit.

As mentioned in a previous chapter, the liberal Left fosters divisiveness. The Left constantly divides people into divergent groups, applies labels to them, and convinces people in those groups that they are victims. Most conservatives don't dwell on the victim/villain mentality as do those on the liberal side. Of course, the Left would respond with "Well, that's because they have all the money and they aren't victims." No, the answer is because conservatives don't believe in the victim/villain game and would rather see effort and positive behavior rewarded than have an environment in which claiming victimhood is rewarded.

Liberals tend to be emotional and heed more of what appeals to their sensitivities than that which appeals to common sense. This is true of educated and intelligent progressives as well as the uneducated and uninformed who gravitate to emotional appeal. Often both choose to believe that which they wish were so rather than that which is so. Politicians on the Left are adept at using that tendency to sell much that simply isn't so.

There are many mistruths perpetuated by the Left to convince people that they are better taken care of by the progressive liberals of the Democrat party. The Left does not like to be described as what they really are. They don't want labels pinned on them that may describe them as less than their idealistic notion of what they think they are. Many now prefer to call themselves progressive to avoid some of the negativity associated with the term liberal.

There are many other examples of reality not matching what progressive liberals like to say. Here are some of them.

<u>According to the Left:</u>

Bill Clinton and the Democrats were responsible for the economic prosperity of the latter half of his presidency.

<u>Why that Isn't Accurate:</u>

Remember that the president cannot make law; that is the function of Congress. Many uninformed people credit (or blame) the president for success (or failure) that should rightly be ascribed to Congress. During Bill Clinton's first two years (January 1991–January 1993), the Democrats were in control of Congress. That liberal Congress imposed tax increases and failed to improve the economy. That and the miserable failure of Bill and Hillary's attempt at health care reform led the American people to put the Republicans in control of Congress in the November 1994 elections. Republicans had the majority in the House of Representatives for the remaining six years of the Clinton administration. Remember Newt Gingrich and his "Contract with America," a policy designed to fix the economy? It was the Republicans in Congress who promoted the legislation that fueled the nice run of prosperity during that time.

Bill Clinton was a clever politician. With an eye on public opinion at all times, he understood that the people would not react favorably if he vetoed the legislation that the Republicans pushed and the people wanted. He was smart enough to ride the wave and take credit for that which he never would have proposed.

Another factor contributing to economic growth during that time was the technology explosion and the Internet. If you buy the ridiculous boast of Al Gore that he "invented the Internet," then perhaps you can justify chalking one up for the Democrats. Of course, had that been true, I think perhaps Al Gore would be in Bill Gates' shoes.

* * * * * *

According to the Left:

George W. Bush and the Republicans ruined the prosperity that they inherited from Bill Clinton.

Why that Isn't Accurate:

The Left does not choose to admit that the economy was receding before Clinton and Gore left office in January 2001. In fact, the stock market peaked in March 2000, ten months before the end of the Clinton administration, leaving George W. Bush to inherit a sliding economy. This recession was mostly a correction to the vigorous expansion caused by the technology boom. The Left also does not choose to acknowledge that the economy runs in cycles. They believe governmental interference is always necessary. There are always economic corrections to both robust and sickly economies, at least so long as the federal government is careful to avoid over-manipulation (which, of course, the Left cannot do).

With the economy already sliding when President Bush took office in January 2001, the cowardly and murderous attacks on our country occurred on September 11, 2001, which further damaged the American economy. The Dow Jones Industrial Average recorded the biggest one-day and one-week losses in its history immediately following the 9/11 attacks.

Subsequently, President Bush and the Republican Congress introduced what is known as the Bush tax cuts. Remember, during the 2001–2003 Congress, Republicans had the majority in the House, and there was a 50-50 split in the Senate. Any 50-50 tie vote in the Senate is decided by the vote of the vice president, meaning the Republicans held the edge. These tax cuts and other legislation were responsible for restoring the economy, leading to low unemployment, growth, and a robust stock market run up to its record high in November 2007.

Incidentally, the Bush tax cuts were a reduction of income taxes for all income levels, not just for the wealthy, as the Left would like you to think. In fact, based on percentage of taxes paid, lower and middle income taxpayers got a significantly larger tax break. The effect of the tax cuts was to (1) increase business investment and hiring by the higher earners, thus stimulating growth and employment, and (2) put more dollars in the hands of the middle and lower earners, which helped them with day-to-day needs and increased purchasing, thus stimulating growth and employment.

The cost of the two wars in Afghanistan and Iraq was a tremendous burden on the federal budget. Such an expense should call for austerity in other areas, but not since World War II have the American people been willing to sacrifice to support a war effort. The Republican-majority Congresses of 2003–2005 and 2005–2007 continued to send too many spending bills to the president.

* * * * * *

<u>According to the Left:</u>

George W. Bush and the Republicans were solely responsible for the economic downturn starting in 2007, which became an economic disaster in 2008.

<u>Why that Isn't Accurate:</u>

The failure of Congress and Bush to control non-Defense spending while funding the wars led to deficit spending and increased debt. The failure of the Republicans to control lending practices advanced by the Left helped lead to the banking crisis and the housing collapse. Perhaps because Republicans and President Bush deemed it politically troublesome to reduce spending, they did not do so. Bush was negligent in not vetoing spending bills sent to him by Congress until after the Democrats took control of Congress. That enabled the Democrats to have their cake and eat it too-continue to fund their progressive Leftist agenda and place all the blame on the Republicans for putting the country in debt.

When Democrats gained control of the House and Senate in January 2007, there was still opportunity to reduce spending and tighten lending practices. Instead, the Democrats continued to support their heavy spending agenda and refused to heed Bush's warnings about the impending banking and housing disaster. It is a fact that Bush asked Congress multiple times to give him legislation to sign that would have significantly lessened the downturn and avoided the collapse.

There are numerous documented instances of both Bush and McCain warning Congress of the looming sub-prime mortgage and banking disaster. It is also on record that highly liberal Democrats Barney Frank, Chuck Schumer, Chris Dodd, and others argued that Fannie Mae and Freddie Mac were in good shape. Frank tried to insist on expanding, rather than reining in, sub-prime loans extended to borrowers who could not afford them.

During Bush's last year in office, the Democrats did nothing to assist the president in saving the economy. Instead, they adopted the most insidious policy of allowing the economy to tank, knowing enough of the gullible public would blame Bush, not them. The Nancy Pelosi House and the Harry Reid Senate simply held out until they could get one of their own, either Hillary Clinton or Barack Obama, elected. They abdicated the responsibility of stopping the collapse in favor of gaining complete control of the legislative and executive branches, allowing the liberal Democrats to advance their agenda. The Democrat Congress refused to take the obvious steps to do what was best for the country, choosing to sacrifice the economy for the sake of gaining political power for themselves and the Left.

So, in a nutshell, the economic collapse was caused by the following:

- Progressive liberal spending measures pushed by Democrats.

- The failure of the Republican Congress to control those measures.

- The failure during 2001–2007 of President Bush to veto excessive spending.

- The Democrats' deceit and sinister strategy of refusing to take action, as Bush strongly advised and requested, to stop the disaster.

So the truth is there is plenty of blame to spread around. It is extremely hypocritical and outright lying for the Left to place the blame solely on President Bush. Certainly he failed to control spending until it was too late (meaning until the Democrats took control of Congress), but his lawmakers, both Republican- and Democrat-controlled Congresses, more than share the blame.

It is irresponsible, divisive, and destructive that the Democrats and President Obama continue, even two years after Bush's departure, to insist that the state of the economy is all Bush's doing. It is appalling that so many Americans believe it. The Obama administration and the Democrat Congress of 2009–2011 are clearly responsible for increasing the deficit more than threefold, increasing unemployment, continuing to burden businesses and stifle economic growth, and quite likely bankrupting the country.

* * * * * *

According to the Left:

When there is economic crisis, government intervention is the best answer.

Why that Is Not Accurate:

Every time the economy takes a downturn and the federal government responds by increasing spending, raising taxes, or creating new programs, the result is a retardation of the normal tendency of the private sector to correct itself. If left alone to manage itself, private enterprise usually reacts in a way that minimizes the negative impact of the down cycle.

We have already mentioned how the massive expansion by FDR in response to the depression of the 1930s actually impeded growth and recovery. At that time, most of the world was in similar economic distress. Those nations that resisted government intervention in the market actually recovered from the depression faster than the United States.

Later, Lyndon Johnson and his Great Society programs did not create a great economy, but instead impeded growth. Jimmy Carter's answer to a slow economy was to create more government and raise taxes. As a result, the economy went into stagflation, a term for little or no economic growth along with higher prices, the worst of both worlds. Interest rates were astronomical during that time, with fixed rate home loans exceeding 15 percent. The only way most people could buy a house was by using adjustable rate mortgages, which often put people into situations they could not afford, a practice we now know is destructive.

President Eisenhower refused to intervene in the marketplace when faced with a mild recession; the result was a fairly quick recovery and a return to a healthy economy. Ronald Reagan's tax cuts and refusal to increase the size of government took us out of the disaster of Carter's policies and sparked the country's record run of prosperity. When the economy naturally slowed at the end of the Reagan run, President George H. W. Bush did not respond by increasing government intervention; thus the downturn was minor. As discussed earlier, President George W. Bush, when faced with a downturn he inherited, responded not by raising taxes and increasing intervention but by cutting taxes. The result, as we know, was a return to prosperity.

Expansions and contractions happen naturally in a capitalistic environment. It is not only natural but healthy. With prudent adjustments of federal monetary policy, the economy will correct itself much more quickly and with much less expense than when the government intervenes by raising taxes and creating new programs. Our history is replete with examples that support this fact.

Remember the famous words of President Ronald Reagan: "In our present crisis, government is not the solution to the problem; government is the problem."

And this one: "The ten scariest words in the English language are 'We're the federal government and we're here to help you.'"

* * * * * *

According to the Left:

The greed of capitalists sends jobs overseas.

Why that Is Not Accurate:

Market forces dictate that companies minimize the expense of doing business. If labor costs and business taxes and restrictions are lower in Asian, South American, or other countries than in the United States, it is predictable that companies will seek the lower costs.

Progressive liberalism has put so many burdens on capitalism to operate in the United States that it forces companies to move jobs overseas. The policies of the state of California are examples of how restricting private enterprise results in corporations moving their business elsewhere.

Big labor unions, political correctness, discriminatory hiring and promoting practices, and an entitlement attitude, all promoted by the Left, drive up production costs. Yes, I did say discrimination fostered by the Left. Progressive liberal practices inhibit hiring and promoting based on credentials and performance, instead based on their idea of equality.

Remember that the US corporate tax rate is 35 percent while the average in other industrialized countries is 19 percent. It is the progressive Left that advocates this high corporate tax rate. It is the policies of the American progressive Left, not those of capitalistic conservatives, that sends jobs abroad.

* * * * * *

<u>According to the Left:</u>

The Left cares about the environment while the capitalists on the Right are irresponsible and criminal in their disregard for the planet because of their greedy pursuit of profits.

<u>Why that Is Not Accurate:</u>

Most worthwhile environmental legislation has had bipartisan support and has achieved compliance from the corporate community. American factories and businesses operate more responsibly than those in most other nations. There is no question that the need for environmental awareness and protection exists, and certainly many environmental policies have produced the desired beneficial effect. However, as with many causes of the Left, the element of alarmism trumps the influence of common sense.

Protection of the environment is a cause that liberals love to claim as theirs alone. Their so-called protection of the globe is largely a sham. What their policies have developed is a bureaucratic system of stupidity. Many of their policies take rights from property owners and prevent energy independence, which is utterly irresponsible. We have environmental policies that support the pet projects of small alarmist groups, to the extent of utter silliness at times. When the government takes away property owners' rights in order to protect certain species of insects, we've gone too far. When the government tells a rancher he can't graze cattle on his own land because his land is a potential habitat for an animal that has never been seen in the area, we've gone too far. When we tell property owners they can't protect their seaside land from erosion (for some reason that escapes me), we've gone too far.

Liberals will point to disasters, such as the BP Gulf oil spill, as evidence of the reckless greed of large corporations and the need for tight government control. While there is plenty of blame to lay at the feet of BP, demonizing the oil industry and shutting down new drilling is the wrong answer. Certainly controls should be in place that provide for the ability to cap leaks. Those controls need to be mutually developed and policed by the government and industry.

Perhaps, if drilling were allowed closer to shore, where the water is much shallower, it would be far easier to control leaks when they occur. Perhaps, if we were allowed to tap the vast petroleum resources available in Alaska and the Dakotas, we could reduce our dependence on Middle Eastern oil, thus improving our position relative to those other oil-producing countries. Liberal environmentalists parade alarmism about perceived damage to the ecosystem and prevent accessing these needed resources.

On matters of individual environmental care, the actions of many liberals belie their words. Personally, I see more day-to-day conservationism practiced by conservatives than by liberals. By nature, conservatives tend to be frugal and conscientious. Frugality leads to waste reduction, which of course benefits the environment. Conservatives tend to be self-reliant and opposed to the bigger role of government promoted by liberals. In this context, that translates to conservatives picking up after themselves and not looking for the government to do it for them.

The conservative nature is to be practical, save money, make things last, plan and schedule, and "waste not, want not," as Benjamin Franklin famously said. A conservative may own an SUV or a big truck but is more likely to conserve fuel by using that vehicle to carry things, combine errands into single trips, and generally act frugally toward the expense of fuel.

Elitist progressive liberals consider themselves far more enlightened than anyone to their Right. They blame others, such as conservatives, for the alleged destruction of the air, water, forests, ice caps, and plant and animal life. It makes progressives feel good about themselves to be seen in a hybrid car and to be considered concerned about global warming and other issues.

Given the massive pollution pumped into the environment by industries in China, India, and emerging third world countries, the liberals' hybrid car demonstration is of little consequence. Instead of blaming American business and condemning conservatives who do actually care about the environment, progressive liberals should be focusing their criticism on those other countries and on people who expect someone else to pick up after them.

Most of us have heard the comparison of the "carbon footprint" of Al Gore with that of George Bush. The irony should slap one in the face but is unfortunately lost on most liberals. Acknowledgment of facts by the Left is just not important, particularly when it debunks their myths. By the way, I wonder how Nancy Pelosi's carbon footprint stacks up against, say, John Boehner's. Consider Speaker Pelosi's insistence on using a large Air Force jet, instead of the usual smaller private jet, for her weekly commute between California and Washington.

When I see someone litter, my instinct is to make the admittedly unjust assumption that it is a person who would vote with the liberals. I associate acts like littering with ignorance and the notion that it is someone else's responsibility to pick up trash, and of course that is what I observe to be the entitlement attitude so prevalent on the Left.

* * * * * *

According to the Left:

The progressive Left is not racist, but the conservative Right is. The Left promotes inclusiveness; the Right does not.

Why that Is Not Accurate:

This is probably the biggest lie of them all. There is no factual support for this absurd notion that liberals continue to trot out in their effort to control the minority vote. If anything, I observe more racism and bias among both white and minority liberals than I do among white and minority conservatives.

Take a close look at the record of President Bush relative to appointing blacks, women, and Hispanics to positions within his administration. It compares very favorably to any previous president, including Democrats Clinton, Carter, Johnson, and Kennedy.

In the free market system advocated by conservatives, blacks and other minorities obtain more jobs. In the big government system advocated by progressive liberals, more people, especially blacks and other minorities, rely on welfare and other subsidies. The private enterprise system provides for self-help and job creation; the big government system is a form of enslavement.

Practically any business owner, large or small, would offer a job or a promotion to the person whom the owner believes is best able to make the business successful. No other decision makes sense. What is racist or sexist about that?

There is so much falsehood spread by the Left on the subject or racism. Liberals like to glad-hand minorities and minority causes and support policies that promise to help those groups. What they get, though, often is more hurtful than helpful. My opinion is that most white liberals don't care about their minority friends as much as they would have you think.

Many black Americans have almost nothing in common with Barack Obama or other progressive elitist blacks. They certainly do not benefit from the policies of Obama and the progressives, unless one has a very low view of what it means to benefit. It should be obvious that more black Americans prosper in the work force under policies that favor private enterprise, but apparently it is not.

In the 2008 presidential election, 55 percent of white voters chose McCain and 43 percent chose Obama. Meanwhile, 95 percent of blacks voted for Obama and 4 percent voted for McCain. We have discussed the tendency of the poor, uninformed, and those considering themselves victims to vote Democrat. That and the heavy influence of the biased media explain why the majority of blacks usually vote Democrat. Of course we all recognize the pride that black Americans must feel to see a man of color become president of the United States, when not so long ago that was impossible. But 95 percent? Isn't that racist?

Those election statistics support an opinion of mine that is admittedly based on observation, an opinion I do not have data to support. It is this: most white conservatives would vote for a black conservative opposing a white liberal, based on values. However, most black liberals would vote for a black candidate opposing a white candidate, regardless of values, based on race.

Personally, I would vote for Allen West (newly elected black congressman from Florida) or Tim Scott (newly elected black congressman from South Carolina) over practically any other candidate of any race or ethnicity. I would also support blacks like Thomas Sowell (prominent writer, columnist, and intellectual), Condoleezza Rice (female Secretary of State under George W. Bush), Herman Cain (prominent political commentator and radio personality), and many others over almost anyone. That should belie the standard liberal assertion that anyone opposing Obama does so because of race rather than the issues.

Of course, the accusation of mainstream liberal blacks toward these accomplished Americans is that they are Uncle Toms, blacks who cater to the white community for their own self-interests. They treat these conservative blacks as traitors, but traitors to what? I assume they are regarded as traitors to the liberal dependence on big government, heavy taxation, and the enslavement of entitlement.

Despite the erosion of Obama's popularity, he may still manage to be nominated to run for another term in 2012. Unless a black Republican emerges, Obama would be opposed by a white Republican. If the country turns against Obama and a significant majority of whites vote for the white candidate against Obama, will liberal Democrats scream racism?

The Left panders to the minority black vote by continuing to apologize for the slave-owning practices of more than 150 years ago and continuing to make purported racism an issue. Slavery was a shameful event in our history, but it is long gone. Regardless, white liberals continue to make it an issue in order to keep the support of the black population. Black liberals continue to make it an issue as a means to make money and deflect attention from, while denying responsibility for, real problems in the black community.

The American liberal Left loves to bash America for the slavery of the past. The truth is, slavery existed worldwide for centuries, and America was certainly not the worst abuser. Slavery was widespread from the earliest recorded history until the nineteenth century, when practically all slavery was abolished. Today, there is virtually no slavery outside of parts of the Muslim world, mostly in Africa.

The Left works at keeping alive the idea of a racial divide that would not be nearly as significant otherwise. So long as white progressives and black activists keep telling blacks that they are discriminated against and taken advantage of by whites, we will have divisiveness.

Any American should realize that organizations whose membership is based on race are, by definition, racist. The most prominent organizations that have those restrictions in America today are black organizations. Most conservatives would tell you that the existence of those organizations is wrong; many liberals support the existence of those organizations to keep alive the separateness.

* * * * * *

According to the Left:

The Left cares more for those less fortunate than do those on the Right. Liberals are more charitable than conservatives.

Why that Is Not Accurate:

The facts show that the opposite is true. Every measurement of charitable giving and charitable actions shows that conservative Americans are far more giving than liberals. The difference is quite significant and is not limited to religious giving. Conservatives give considerably more to secular charitable organizations than do liberals.

Conservatives give more and do more to help those who need it. This is not because conservatives have more money to give. On comparative levels of income, all across the board, conservatives give more of their money than do liberals. The discrepancy in the charitable giving of political candidates over the past decade between that of conservatives and that of liberals is significant.

Part of the reason for more generosity among conservatives is based on religion, but much of it is based on the conservative values of self-help and assistance to others, unlike the tendency of liberals to always look elsewhere for assistance. My observation is that conservatives are more generous with their own time and money, whereas liberals tend to be more generous with someone else's time and money.

The Left prefers using wealth redistribution through taxation to care for those who need help. The societal effect of their government entitlement programs is more destructive than helpful. The liberal Left's policy of caring for those who have children out of wedlock increases the number of children born out of wedlock. Their policy of increasing welfare, food stamps, and other payments to those who ask for them increases the number of people on welfare, food stamps, or other assistance. Their policy of insisting that everyone should have a fine home increases the number of foreclosures on people who buy homes they cannot afford.

The progressive liberal policy of increased taxation and intervention erodes the ability and the incentive to be charitable. It is more difficult to contribute when so much is gouged out of your paycheck by the federal government.

* * * * * *

According to the Left:

The economic plight of lower and middle income people increases because of the wealthy-favoring policies of the conservative Right.

Why that Is Not Accurate:

This is another favorite of the Left because it convinces many lower and middle class voters that their economic interests are best represented by Democrats. The facts reveal something else entirely. The standard of living of lower and middle income earners was higher in the mid-2000s, after a decade of Republican majority in the House and after the Bush tax cuts, than ever before. Furthermore, the percentage of income taxes paid by middle income earners after the Bush tax cuts was half that paid during the Carter administration (when, by the way, Democrats were enjoying a long run of control of both the House and Senate).

The Left likes to point out that the middle class is shrinking because of Republican policies under presidents like Bush. They claim these policies favor the wealthy at the expense of the middle class. This is another way to twist the truth to lead people into thinking they are victims.

The truth is that the shrinking of the middle class is a result of two things. One is that more people from the middle class are moving upward, not downward. The middle class of thirty or more years ago lived in homes today's middle class would not consider. The middle class homes in which many of my generation grew up would be considered poverty level today. The middle class of the past did not have the consumer products, the automobiles, and the standard of living of today's middle class.

The second reason is the expanding of the entitlement class. A significantly larger number of people qualify for greater amounts of entitlement handouts, thus reducing the incentive to work and strive for the middle class.

The evidence, not the liberal rhetoric, indicates workers at all levels of income do better with conservative fiscal policy and smaller government. The big government advocated by the Left, with its promised help for the underprivileged, is demonstrably more destructive to their well-being.

* * * * * *

According to the Left:

There is a substantial Fascist, or Nazi-like, element on the conservative Right.

Why that Is Not Accurate:

Along with trying to paint conservatives as racist, another favorite mantra among liberals is to try to associate Nazi dogma with Republicans. The civilized world views Hitler's nazism as an evil blight in world history, so liberals love to try to make that association. While there is certainly an element of idiots that identify with nazism while associating with the political Right, they exert no influence among conservatives.

The truth is that Adolph Hitler actually admired some of the precepts of communism as advanced by Lenin and Mao, particularly the notion of the government having control of industry and the limiting of individual liberty. Nazism is unusual in that it embraces some of what is typical among far Right conservatives and reactionaries while also assuming many of the precepts of the radical Left. To put fascism in the camp with conservatism is illogical and inaccurate.

If anything, it is the Left that uses the Nazi tactic of pitting groups of citizens against each other, fomenting hatred and unfounded blame. The modern Left cultivates those emotions to sustain animosity toward conservatives in a way strangely similar to what Hitler did toward Jews.

6

What the Left Does

The majority on the Left vehemently insist they and their policies are not socialist. However, Western secular progressive liberalism does indeed approximate the ideals of socialism. Socialism oppresses the common person and promotes policy that does not care about individualism or individual rights. Socialism does not support much of what is written in the United States Constitution. Socialists are totalitarians who favor the government deciding what is best for the individual.

Wikipedia, the online free encyclopedia, has this definition of totalitarianism, with which I agree:

> Totalitarianism is a political system where the state, usually under the control of a single political person, faction, or class, recognizes no limits to its authority and strives to regulate every aspect of public and private life wherever feasible. Totalitarian regimes or movements maintain political power through an all-encompassing campaign of propaganda disseminated through the state-controlled mass media, a single party that is often

marked by personality cultism, control over the economy, regulation and restriction of speech, mass surveillance, and widespread use of state terrorism.

Does that sound a bit like what we've seen from Washington lately? Let me add parenthetical comments to this definition to illustrate the totalitarian behavior of the progress liberal Left and the Obama administration.

Totalitarianism is a political system where the state (under the control of the president and progressive liberals), recognizes no limits to its authority and strives to regulate every aspect of public and private life wherever feasible. Totalitarian regimes or movements maintain political power through an all-encompassing campaign of propaganda (misrepresentations of their intent and slander of the opposition), disseminated through the state controlled mass media (mainstream liberal media), a single party (the progressive Democrat party) that is often marked by personality cultism (the love affair of progressives and the liberal media with the persona of Barack Obama), control over the economy (takeover of all or much of the banking, automotive, college loan, and other industries, most notably health care), mass surveillance (or intervention into personal liberties and personal decision-making), and widespread use of state terrorism (alarmism, blame-laying, animosity, race-baiting, creation of victim and entitlement mentalities, and threats).

There is certainly a case for the assertion that the policies and position of the present administration and the 111th Congress approach totalitarian rule. Incidentally, the most notable totalitarians in modern history were Joseph Stalin and Adolph Hitler. There are certainly similarities between the actions and attitudes of totalitarians and those of the progressive liberal Left. Despite what progressives like to say, that is not true of conservatives, libertarians, or Tea Partiers.

* * * * * *

We know there are Democrats who are moderate, even conservative, who represent fairly conservative districts or states. We would like to believe them when they campaign on their principles. Unfortunately, the political system today is such that conservative Democrats are squashed by the progressive liberal leadership of their party. If a moderate or conservative Democrat opposes a progressive liberal measure, the party is quick to apply pressure. It's like this: if you don't vote with the party, you'll never get anything you propose out of committee. The pressure to cave in and go with the flow of the party is enormous. Thus the concept of voting for "the person, not the party" is largely invalidated.

Progressive liberals favor the involvement of the federal government in as much as possible. They take power away from the individual and the states and give it to the federal government. They use this power to control who benefits from what services and who pays for those services. The size, cost, and influence of the federal government increase when the progressive Left is in control of Congress. That is what they do.

Democrats raise taxes to support the increased spending necessary to fund the progressive takeover of the economy. They continue to insist they only want to raise taxes on the highest incomes while passing measure after measure that increases taxes on all incomes. When Obama campaigned for office, he insisted that only people making over a certain amount of money would see a tax increase. His position since being elected is quite different. There are simply not enough wealthy people to provide for all the programs of the Left, so they must tax everyone. The Left's desire to let the Bush tax cuts expire would result in a significant tax increase for all citizens who pay taxes. The percentage increase will be greater on the lower tax rates than on those of the wealthiest. What about some of the other dozen or so tax increases inside those multi-thousand-page bills?

Let's do a little math to illustrate the effect of raising taxes. Assume there is an employee of a private business that earns a salary of $60,000 a year. Assume the additional cost paid by the employer for that person is another $20,000. If the company must make an operating profit of 10 percent to justify being in business, this employee's work must be responsible for adding around $88,000 to the company's income or the position does not pay for itself.

Let's further assume that this employee pays $12,000 in federal income tax plus Social Security and Medicare deductions, leaving the employee with $48,000 in take-home pay. (Let's leave state income tax out of the equation, inasmuch as not all states tax employees' incomes and for the sake of simplification.) There is a gap of $40,000 between what the employer must make to justify this employee and what the employee takes home.

Let's raise taxes by a little bit, both on the "rich" employer and on the employee. Instead of the highest tax rate of 35 percent (the Bush tax cut rate), the business owner's new rate is 39.6 percent (the old highest rate under Clinton). That is an increase in taxes of 13 percent on the employer. The company's income must increase by about $1,000 to pay for this one employee.

Let's also increase the personal income tax on the employee by about $800, the approximate effect of letting the Bush tax cuts expire. The bottom line now is that the company must make $89,000 in order for this employee to now take home $47,200, a gap of $41,800.

The two consequences of this progressive liberal policy of raising taxes are that (1) the employee has $800 less to spend in the economy, and (2) the company must raise its prices by 1 percent or so or find a way to reduce its costs by that percentage. The employee consumer has less money to purchase the goods or services provided by the employer's (or some other) company.

The tax hike created a decrease in aggregate demand coupled with a need to raise prices. Those two forces are in direct conflict. With decreased demand, there is pressure on the company to reduce, not increase, prices, so the employer's only option is to reduce costs. Reducing costs usually means eliminating jobs.

* * * * *

Common sense would suggest that the government not spend more than it takes in. When the government spends more than it has, that creates a budget deficit. Continuing deficits increase the national debt. The concept of deficits and debt at the federal government level is hardly more complicated than at the basic family level.

Let's assume a couple got married and started their first year of marriage with no debt and no savings. Let's say together they earned $50,000 in their first year but spent $55,000. That means the couple operated at a deficit of $5,000 in the first year, thereby creating a debt of $5,000.

How can they do this? By borrowing, of course: loans, credit cards, other borrowing. Now what happens? First, the debt must be repaid along with interest, so that repayment is added to the expenses. Now they must either reduce their spending or increase their income, or they will increase their annual deficit.

Suppose their income and their spending don't change in the next year. In the second year they must take on the added expense of, say, $1,000 as payment, including principle and interest, on the loans and credit cards. So now they have added $1,000 to their expenses and created a deficit of $6,000 in the second year.

Assume that in making payments on year one's $5,000 debt, they paid off $600 of the debt (the other $400 was interest on the debt), so they have reduced the first year debt down to $4,400. But, since they continued the same spending habits in the second year, at the end of it their debt is $6,000 plus $4,400 = $10,400, more than double what it was after year one. Now their debt burden is much greater. If they don't do something, it won't take all that long to go bankrupt.

This, in simple terms, is what our federal government has done: take us down the road to bankruptcy. The federal government is just like that family, spending more than it takes in, creating a deficit, and piling up debt.

Sometimes, to avoid more borrowing when it has spent too much, the government simply creates more money by printing it. It's easy to see what happens when more money is printed. Like anything else, where there is more of something, each individual part is less valuable. So the value of the dollar goes down, which has negative consequences domestically and in the global financial community.

* * * * *

Consider the consequences of creating more and more government jobs. As the government increases in size, it creates a bigger payroll burden. Remember that the government does not sell goods and services to generate income—it only taxes those who do. As the government gets bigger, the percentage of people working within the government increases, creating a larger and larger need for payroll money from a smaller and smaller percentage of people who work outside the government and pay taxes to it.

As expansion of the government continues, the ability of the populace to afford it decreases. The only way for the government to continue to grow at a greater rate than the growth of the private sector economy, regardless of whether or not it raises taxes, is to go into more and more debt. The government cannot continue to find ways to accumulate more debt indefinitely. At some point, the piper must be paid.

Let's do some math to examine what increasing the size of the government does:

Consider that private business employee who makes $60,000 per year and pays $12,000 in federal income taxes, Social Security, and Medicare. Assume there is a federal employee who does the same job at the same pay for a government agency and pays the same amount in taxes. Assume the cost of benefits for this government employee, including funding retirement, is another $30,000, for a total cost to the taxpayer of $90,000 a year.

Since the government employee contributes $12,000 in taxes, the remaining $78,000 cost of the government employee must be paid by the taxpayers in the private sector. Given the $12,000 in taxes paid by our private enterprise worker above, it would take 6.5 such private employees to pay for this one government worker. And that doesn't leave any money from those 6.5 workers to pay other federal government expenses.

It would be interesting to measure the positive economic effect of those 6.5 private sector workers compared to that of the one public servant. Obviously, reducing the number of government employees, thereby leaving more money in the private sector, would be a great boost to the economy.

* * * * *

There isn't much question that our country was founded on the principles that each citizen should have the same opportunity to "life, liberty, and the pursuit of happiness." That is not the same as saying everyone is equal. People are not equal. We all have different talents, abilities, and interests, and certainly different levels of incentive and determination.

Surely no American would argue against the idea that everyone should have equal opportunity, as the founding fathers intended. However, there is a lot of disagreement about what equal opportunity means. Denying equal treatment because of race, ethnicity, gender, religion, or other such criteria is obviously wrong. However, that doesn't mean every person is capable of, or deserving of, the same things as every other person.

Social and political progressives push for equality. To them, it is not enough to remove barriers to equal opportunity. Based on their notion that everyone is entitled to the same things as everyone else, progressives want to ensure that those in their identified "victim" groups get what the others have.

There was a photo going around the Internet that showed Michele Obama helping out at a soup kitchen. In line waiting for his free meal was a guy taking a picture of Mrs. Obama with his very expensive-looking Blackberry. That's the kind of opportunity we now provide in this country: the opportunity to get welfare meals while owning a several-hundred-dollar advanced electronic device.

Liberals tend to support programs that provide taxpayer money for things like college education and home ownership, even for those who don't really need to be going to college and those who can't afford the mortgage payments on the home they get assistance to purchase. Everyone should have the same opportunity to a college education, based on qualifications. That does not mean that everyone should have the *right* to a college education. Everyone should have the same opportunity to purchase a home, qualify for financing, and live in any area they choose and can afford. That does not mean everyone has the *right* to own a home.

Further, why should one citizen have to pay, through taxes, to provide these things for those who cannot (or at least say they cannot) afford them? Why should a young person who chooses not to go to college, but instead enters the work world learning a trade or business, have to pay, through more taxes, for someone else to go to college? Why should a couple who plans and sacrifices for years in advance to build savings for their child's tuition have to pay, through more taxes, for someone else's child to go to college? Why should anyone have to pay taxes so that the federal government can underwrite and then absorb bad home loans?

Progressive liberals believe everyone should have the right to higher education, health care, housing, jobs, and material possessions. A conservative would argue that everyone should enjoy the *opportunity* to the same possessions, education, and advantages available to anyone. No one should be denied obtaining those things based on anything other than ability and the means to pay for them. However, no one should be given these things at others' expense just because others have them.

Because we all have different abilities, ambitions, and backgrounds, the path to success is easier for some than for others. That's the way it is, but progressives consider that unfair, and thus they must tilt the playing field to make sure their "victims" are not denied anything. The means to accomplish that is, of course, to transfer money from those who have it to those who don't and to demand inequitable practices in lending and hiring.

Often, the liberal effort to make things fair has an effect quite the opposite of what was intended. Consider the minimum wage.

To most of us who work, the minimum wage is not very much of an income. Certainly, we wouldn't want to get out of bed and go work for an income that won't support us. Thus it feels right to support the government raising the minimum wage.

There are some problems, though, that proponents of higher minimum wages either ignore or don't realize. What happens when the minimum wage is raised? One effect is to dampen hiring by small business owners who cannot pay much for some menial tasks. Regardless of whether or not a particular worker might be willing to work for lesser pay, the government won't let it happen.

It has been shown that when the minimum wage is raised, one effect is the loss of jobs available at the bottom of the wage scale. The most negatively affected group of workers is young blacks. It is shown that every time the minimum wage is increased, there in an increase in young black unemployment. How's that for the benevolence of mandating higher minimum wages? Another effect is the massive shift of menial jobs being done by illegal aliens, instead of citizens, and the movement of jobs overseas.

When government policy strives for equality, as distinguished from liberty (equal opportunity), what results is hardly what is intended. Rather than achieving the desired level field, the effect is to *increase* unfairness. Policies introduced by the government in an effort to produce some utopian equality have instead devalued personal achievement and created a sense of entitlement.

Progressive liberals would like to have the reputation of caring about the individual. However, the result of their actions is quite the contrary. They stand against individual liberty, individual decision-making, and individual thinking. Notice how often they seek to restrict individual choices. The progressive Left is constantly trying to modify individual behavior to conform to its socialist thinking.

* * * * *

As mentioned earlier, the progressive liberal policies of the Left polarize people, reinforcing the victim mentality that insists on entitlement. Those policies promote distrust and disharmony among citizens.

The result, and perhaps intent, of the liberal need to typecast conservatives as racists, chauvinists, and homophobes is divisiveness. Conservatives do not rant on and on about the differences among Americans the way liberals do. Conservatives would rather acknowledge that we are all Americans and deserve equal opportunity to what America has to offer. Liberals don't recognize the homogeneity of Americans; they constantly bring up the differences. You cannot just be an American to a progressive liberal, treated the same as all Americans. You must be a black or African American, a Latin or Hispanic American, a woman, a gay American, or some other minority group. Furthermore, if you're in one of those groups, you surely must be discriminated against.

Barack Obama delivered a very impassioned and eloquent speech at the 2004 Democratic National Convention, an appearance that thrust him into the national limelight and made him a contender for the 2008 presidential election. In this speech, Obama made these statements that we should all embrace:

"There's not a liberal America and a conservative America; there's the United States of America. There's not a black America and white America and Latino America and Asian America; there's the United States of America."

Contrast that message with these two remarks by Obama in the last few days before the 2010 elections:

"We don't mind the Republicans joining us. They can come for the ride, but they have to sit in back." (President Obama's remarks at the Democratic Congressional Campaign Committee reception in Providence, RI, on October 25, 2010.)

"If Latinos sit out the election instead of saying, 'We're going to punish our enemies and we're going to reward our friends who stand with us on issues that are important to us…'" (Radio interview remarks aired on Univision on October 25, 2010.)

These are but two small examples of the rhetoric used by the liberal Left to continue to fan the flames of animosity and separateness. They are quite contrary to those grand remarks Obama made in 2004. The United States has become dangerously polarized under Democrat leadership. This is in direct contradiction to the campaign promise Obama made in 2008 to unite the country.

Rather than being the party of inclusiveness, liberal Democrats are the party of divisiveness. The obvious explanation lies in the need for Democrats to keep alive the mostly false idea that discrimination against so-called minority groups is alive and practiced by conservatives. Those too ignorant or too unwilling to understand reality continue to believe this liberal lie.

The result of this divisiveness is that Democrats continue to get the large majority of the black, Hispanic, and gay vote, and an often significant majority of the female vote. It is not a far-fetched analogy to compare how liberal Democrats keep the fires of distrust and animosity stoked to the methods used by the likes of Hitler, Mao, Lenin, and Stalin.

* * * * *

Progressive liberals are destroyers, often without realizing it. Their policy and practices destroy self-reliance, independence, incentive, and human dignity, while creating nothing (other than more government and a false notion of hope).

They loudly express their support of the First Amendment right to freedom of speech, but their actions do quite the opposite. Their defense of this right is only applied to speech that agrees with theirs, not that of their adversaries. This dichotomy goes hand in hand with their ludicrous notion of political correctness. It is always one-dimensional. Their view is that it is inappropriate or outrageous for non-progressives to express an opinion that they deem offensive, with no regard for the truthfulness of the remark. Meanwhile, they have no compunction about making unfounded accusations of racism against those who disagree with them.

* * * * *

Ron Ewart, president of the National Association of Rural Landowners (www.narlo.org), a nonprofit organization dedicated to defending the rights and interests of property owners, has written extensively on the unconstitutional actions of progressive liberal Democrats. In his article published in the *Canada Free Press*, August 29, 2008, entitled "Democrats Are Traitors to America's Founding Principles of Freedom and Liberty," he wrote the following:

> The Democrats since FDR and his New Deal have served up to the American people a platter of abject socialism and now, radical environmentalism. The American people have been bought, sold and conquered on the promises and propaganda of Democrats who have raided the public treasury for the sole purpose of buying votes to remain in power. They have accomplished this takeover with a cultural mindset that bears no relation to constitutional principles. They have appealed to the weakness in men that buy into the hype, propaganda, lies and distortions

of these con men in order to receive these so-called "free" benefits from their government that bear no relation to their labors. All this the Democrats have done, without a shot being fired.

In almost every word and deed, Democrats have forsaken our Constitution, even though Democrat politicians swear on sacred oath to preserve, protect and defend that very same Constitution. They counter with, "the Constitution is a 'fluid' document, subject to interpretation that changes over time." They ignore the statements in the Constitution that mandate it to be the Supreme Law of the Land and to be literally construed using the original intent of the Framers.

Democrats apologize to the rest of the world for our achievements. We have allowed their socialist and radical environmental agendas to pervade our lives, usurp our rights and trash our Constitution. We have allowed the infiltration of their unconstitutional agendas into our national culture.

They apologize for our greatness to the rest of the world. They have buried our well-deserved national pride in their attempts to seek approval from other countries with failed and corrupt governments. Democrats have capitulated to the whims of foreign nations because those nations don't like our policies of freedom for every corner of the world; policies that we know lead to self-reliance, productivity and peace. Unashamedly, Democrats appease our enemies.

Internally, we have allowed the Democrats to turn our balance of power, designed by our Founding Fathers in the executive, legislative, and judicial branches of government, on its head, and we have allowed un-elected bureaucrats to make our laws. Our bureaucracies have been infiltrated by liberal, socialist and radical environmental graduates out of our very liberal colleges. And these bureaucracies make law, after law, after law until we are sick of laws and end up becoming lawless. Through these laws, with no constitutional authority or legislative approval, they take our land, our money and our rights as individual Americans and we have let them do it.

America needs to be the leader and the shining light to the world, not try to compete with the different forms of government and merge our "ways" with their "ways." We are the most powerful country on earth because we are free. America is and has been a beacon to the world and will continue to be that beacon unless we let Democrats, and others who seek our destruction, try to dim that light with failed policies, negativism, despondency, dependency, the trashing of our Constitution and embarrassment for our achievements, instead of being proud of them. We are great as a country and great as a people because of those achievements.

What America does will determine the fate of the world. If we forsake freedom, if we sell our sovereignty for expediency or a few pieces of silver, if we break the bonds of our Constitution, if we abdicate our right and duty to defend freedom for ourselves and future generations, we shall descend into the mediocrity, apathy and self loathing under which the rest of the world operates and will be pulled down to their level, never to rise again.

We have grave concerns that what we are facing today is a premeditated orchestration of the dismantling of our sacred institutions of freedom by Democrats and international elitists, that find that a free America stands in the way of their distorted concept of the one-world-order, social justice and environmental protection, at any cost. Their unconstitutional give-away policies have this country on the brink of bankruptcy. Their environmental policies of restricting everything that we do, has brought this once-proud, can-do nation to its knees and has forced us to be dependent on other countries for our energy and other vital resources necessary for a thriving economy. Their open-border and amnesty policies that allow anyone to come here illegally will change the color of our politics and thus our freedom, for decades to come, from which we may never recover.

A clear and present danger hangs over this country like a dark, ominous, angry cloud and threatens our freedom, if not our very existence. That dark, black cloud is manifested in abject socialism and radical environmentalism, the twin domestic evils that have invaded every corner of our culture and that have been sold to us by a "liberal" mentality, promoted by Democrats. Their ideas didn't come from our founding principles and our laws, they came out of the bowels of socialist Europe and the United Nations and have been codified into law by Democrat presidential executive orders and a Democrat-controlled US Congress that has lost all allegiance to the Supreme Law of the Land, our Constitution. These policies come at us with soft-sounding words like social equity, compassion, smart growth, sustainable development, biospheres, wildlife corridors, endangered species, invasive species, global warming, mass transit and the one-world order. It's all dressed up in motherhood, apple pie and Chevrolet and it is one of the biggest con games ever perpetrated on what have now become naïve, uninformed Americans.

But today, the hidden agenda of these perpetrators is finally being exposed all across America, as people are waking up to what has happened to them while they were sleeping. It's way past time to fight back. This is still a great country, full of great people, and it is salvageable if we will just vigorously defend our Constitution and hold government to its limits, against the onslaught of failed liberal policies.

Should Barack Hussein Obama be elevated to president of the United States by the electorate because he happens to be a superb speaker, it could easily spell the death knell for a free United States of America. If the electorate is so naïve as to elect a person with no substance and no experience, they shall get what they deserve. If they put this man in office based on hero worship and mass hysteria, the unintended consequences of their actions will reverberate throughout our history for 100 years or more, and our great country may have no chance of ever recovering from the effects of what he and a Democrat-controlled Congress will do.

Democrats are traitors to America's founding principles of freedom and liberty and are willing accomplices to the enemies of our freedom and our sovereignty. Those naïve Democrats who have hitched their wagon to this party aid and abet the destruction of America. No other conclusion is possible.

Unfortunately, Republicans are headed in the same direction and have forsaken their principles of small government, lower taxes and less restrictions on the people that was laid down in a blueprint for free men and women with common purpose and resolve to live out their lives and govern their individual and collective affairs by adhering to that blueprint, some 232 years ago.

I realize that not all voters who call themselves Democrats embrace the radical position of modern progressive liberal Democrats. However, as Ewart points out, "those naïve Democrats ... aid and abet the destruction of America" by voting for those who support the progressive liberal agenda.

* * * * *

To sum it up, most liberals seem to embrace the following:

- A quasi-socialist political model that includes central government control rather than the capitalist and strong local government model on which the country was founded. Liberals do this in spite of all evidence that our economy is strongest, with fuller employment, when government is small, and in spite of all evidence about the societal destruction of socialism.

- Fostering division among various groups of people by constantly pitting one group against another. Liberals do this in utter contradiction of the inclusivity and unity they delude themselves as representing.

- A deep contempt for those who do not share their views, along with the need to justify themselves by denigrating others using extremely negative labels.

- A hatred for conservatism and a disdain for the very values that created and developed this country.

- Various causes that have a "feel-good" ring to them, whether or not those causes make sense. Liberals especially like to embrace causes that seem to protect or promote the perceived underdog, without regard for validity or soundness.

- An assault on Christian and Jewish religious expression while encouraging protection of religious expression among other groups. Liberals somehow are able to rationalize the removing of Christian and Jewish influence while enabling Islamic or other religious influence. This they do in spite of the reality that Christians and Jews are not out to kill Americans, while fundamentalist Muslims are.

- Charisma, eloquence, charm, wit, and idealism, rather than character, sincerity, leadership, common sense, and practicality.

- A rejection of, or misrepresentation of, factual data that do not support their position.

- Abhorrence for military action to the point where appeasement is a nobler option than self-defense.

- A stunning disregard for history, traditional values, the founding principles of our country, and the best interests of the majority.

Liberals take offense when accused of being socialist, anti-American, less patriotic, less supportive of our military, or excessively emotional, hateful, or bigoted. Because many liberals view themselves as noble, enlightened, ethically and morally superior, and humane, they are able to dwell in a world of delusion that protects them from realizing the negative consequences of much of what they say and do.

7

The Left and Business

Liberals continue to advance the idea that business is inherently evil and seeks to make profits to the detriment of the poor. They have created new generations of anti-capitalists who don't understand the value of the profit motive and who see the government as the protector against the Evil Empire of Enterprise.

America did not become the most powerful, successful, and envied nation in the history of the world because the government limited the ability of private business to make money. No, it did so because men and women started and developed businesses, worked for businesses, and profited from businesses.

However, there is an "unholy alliance" among Wall Street insiders, big business, and politicians of both parties. The average liberal Democrat derides the conservative Right for supporting exploitative practices of big business and Wall Street. The politicians don't tell you the real truth. Anyone who doesn't think Wall Street is in bed with Democrats at least as much as with Republicans is deluded. The Barack Obama campaign in 2008 set an all-time record for contributions from Wall Street insiders. In addition, several key Obama staff and cabinet members have Wall Street backgrounds.

Market players stand to gain from liberal Democrat policies, the same policies that hurt the average person. For example, consider the Cap and Trade bill passed by Nancy Pelosi's House in 2009. That legislation would support many careers of insiders who would have a new commodity (energy credits) to trade. Meanwhile, that legislation would drive up utility costs paid by every household as well as the costs of goods and services. Thankfully, that legislation appears to be dead in the Senate with little chance of resurrection.

Large corporations have the money to adapt to heavy regulations and restrictions favored by the liberal Left. Those regulations and restrictions often have the effect of forcing the smaller competitors out of business; they either go bankrupt or are swallowed up by the big boys. Liberal Democrat proposals that appear to the uninformed voter to protect the little guy from the greedy big boys generally produce the opposite result.

It is particularly naïve to think that insiders and the biggest industries suffered because of the banking and housing collapse of 2008. Under the philosophy of "Too Big to Fail," many large companies merely morphed from making money from profits to taking money from the government, which is you, the taxpayer. As always, the ones who suffer are on Main Street, not Wall Street. Many liberals insist that only Republican politicians are involved in the inside dealing of big business and Wall Street. Those liberals are either ignorant or lying.

My discussion below supporting private enterprise is not meant to ignore the corruption, extortion, and taxpayer victimization that are business as usual in Washington. Private enterprise is the backbone of our economy and our advanced culture. We certainly must clean up the bad behavior, but we don't need to kill small and medium-sized businesses to do it. The majority of businesses are small businesses, not large corporations. Raising taxes on business hurts the small ones far more than it does the big ones.

We in the United States enjoy access to more products and services at lower costs than any other nation in the world. Is this because the government made it so, or is it because ambitious people have continued to find more and better ways to produce and sell these products, based upon the motive to make money?

It is popular among progressive liberals to blame capitalism for all manner of evils. They seem to believe there is something wrong with making too much money and wanting to keep most of it. They would insist it is the responsibility of those who make money to give more of that money to the government so that the government can determine how best to use it to help others.

It strikes me as particularly ignorant to want to reduce the incentive for companies to make profits. It doesn't take a genius to understand that profits, while making owners richer, also provide opportunity for others. What does common sense tell you? It tells me that increasing taxes on those who make the most is destructive on several levels. Increasing taxes on the supposed rich means (1) cutting into the ability of businesses to prosper, (2) reducing jobs, (3) undermining the incentive to earn and invest, and (4) reducing research, development, and innovation.

Liberals argue that profits and huge salaries for executives are unfair and greedy. They sell the case to raise taxes on business and on the "rich" as being the right thing to do. Ironically, we don't hear progressives complain about excessive compensation for Hollywood, television, music, and sports entertainers.

The majority of corporate owners are not wealthy executives. The owners are the stockholders, including people who depend on profits (dividends and increase in value) to sustain themselves. These owners include pension plans, insurance companies, investment companies, and individuals like the widow down the street who needs her dividends to supplement her little Social Security check and her meager savings or pension.

My uncle gave me five shares of common stock in a major oil company as a high school graduation present. He encouraged me to reinvest the dividends and let the investment grow. The original five shares have grown over the years to a few hundred shares. Those shares go up and down in value (up over the long haul) and pay modest dividends. Frankly, the ability of my stock to go up in value and pay me some return on my investment, even modestly, depends on the government keeping taxes on the corporate profits at a reasonable level. While my shares make me an owner of a major oil company, I certainly don't see myself getting rich because of it.

Setting arbitrary definitions for who is considered well-compensated (the "wealthy") and increasing taxes on them is particularly misguided. While the average voter might think something like "Yeah, anyone making $250,000 a year is rich and should pay more taxes," that is far from a thoughtful position. Most small business owners making that much or more reinvest their profits back into their business.

It is a misconception that when the rich get richer, the poor get poorer. Using this erroneous notion, the tax-and-spend politicians restrict the ability of successful producers to earn more money and, instead, redistribute that money to those in need. So what's wrong with that? What's wrong with taking from the rich and giving to the poor?

The truth is when the rich get richer, the poor tend to do better, and when the rich get poorer, the poor get even poorer. Why? Because when the rich get richer, it is generally because they are (1) reinvesting and thus stimulating the economy, (2) expanding and creating more jobs, and (3) paying more taxes.

Particularly hardest hit by increased taxes on the so-called wealthy are small businesses. Politicians know that most voters are not wealthy and also know that there is a natural tendency to be envious of those who make more money than you do. Most of us who work hard to barely be able to pay our bills always think, "If I just made X more, I'd be in great shape."

Say you make $40,000 a year and you're just squeezing by (or perhaps going into debt to try to stay ahead of your bills). It's normal to think of someone making more money, such as your supervisor making $60,000 or your manager making $80,000, and say, "Wow, if I made that much, I could get out of debt and have plenty or money." Meanwhile, that $80,000 manager is probably doing the same thing you're doing, perhaps in a little better house and driving a nicer car, saying, "Wow, if I made as much as my $100,000-a-year boss, I'd have it made."

How hard is it for a politician to sell the idea that those who make more money should pay a greater percentage of their income in taxes? How much sympathy do so many uninformed or idealistic people tend to have for those who make more money? It is the consistent position of the liberal Left that those who make more should have more taxes taken from them. Unless you understand how that affects everyone, you might agree.

When taxes are increased, the result is to destimulate the economy. While it sounds caring and noble to ask those who make money to give more to those who don't, it just doesn't work. Taking from those who work and giving to those who don't (but could) is a negative incentive for both sides. It's a job killer and an enabler of the entitlement mentality.

When the government tries to improve the economy by raising taxes, the result is usually increased unemployment and *less* government revenue in the long run. Historically, when the government lowers taxes, unemployment goes down and government revenues go *up*. I wrote earlier that President Bush's tax cuts helped the economy. Here is why:

- Those in the middle and lower income brackets had more money to spend. They spent it and increased the demand for production.

- Those in the upper middle brackets, including small business owners, had more money to spend and saw their sales increase. They were able to hire more workers, thus creating jobs and lowering unemployment.

- Those in the highest brackets, including big business owners, were able to increase capital and production, thus producing more jobs and expanding research and development of new products.

- The tax revenues of the federal government increased because of the stronger economy: more people were working and earning more.

The idea of raising taxes on those greedy, rich corporations has appeal, doesn't it? Certainly there is an element of greed involved in the capitalistic process of making money by providing goods and services. Is the desire to increase one's bank account bad? No, it is what, in part, drives the economic vehicle. As discussed earlier, if you take away the ability to make money, you take away the incentive to own and run a business, yet we tax our businesses in the United States more than practically any other industrialized country.

Any business, large or small, that makes a profit spends that revenue on some combination of the following: expansion (creating more jobs), increasing income for the owners (more income for the government through taxing that income), reducing debt (enabling a healthier banking system), granting raises to employees (more money in the economy), and purchasing more equipment and inventory (stimulating the economy and creating more jobs).

Those who oppose our free enterprise system do not understand (or choose not to recognize) the positive effects of private businesses making money. You hear liberals all the time denigrating capitalism because they think the system rewards the rich at the expense of the poor. They refuse to accept or admit that the system can reward both rich and poor. Those who believe that capitalism is somehow evil (or at least unfair) simply do not understand economics or choose to ignore reality and instead embrace some utopian idea of equality for everyone (spreading the wealth).

The United States taxes its businesses at a higher rate than just about any other industrialized nation. Even so-called socialist countries don't tax their companies as hard as we do. So why do we? Why would anyone want their employer to not make a healthy profit? Who gets a wage or salary increase when the company makes no money?

What about the prices that companies charge for goods and services? In a private enterprise (capitalistic) society, businesses provide goods and services to people, who are free to decide whether or not to purchase those goods and services. A basic component of the decision to buy is price. Setting prices too high will send customers elsewhere. Competition and the free ability of competitors to make their business decisions on the basis of their self-interests produces the lowest prices and most availability to customers. When corporate taxes are raised, the effect has to be a corresponding increase in prices to consumers. Finally, increasing taxes on businesses and on the income of small business owners increases the number of jobs sent overseas.

There are many other taxes, besides income taxes and corporate taxes, that the Left promote in order to tax anything that is successful. They favor an increased capital gains tax rate, increased taxes on dividends, and the particularly destructive estate tax.

This tax, also called the Inheritance Tax or Death Tax, is levied upon someone's estate after that person's death. This tax is not a tax on the dead. It is a tax on the living based on the event of someone's death.

This tax is wrong in so many ways. First of all, the assets that are taxed upon death have already been taxed; inheritance taxation is double taxation. Second, this tax has a negative effect on the economy because it destroys wealth and jobs. Third, this tax has a negative effect on small business. Many small businesses and farms have been lost because the heirs could not afford to pay the taxes and closed or sold the business or farm.

Liberals would argue that this tax only affects the rich. After all, they only want to tax estates of $1 million or greater. That position reflects the ignorance of those who support other taxes on the so-called wealthy. It fails to acknowledge the negative effect on the entire economy.

Consider the many small business owners and farmers who may have assets worth a couple of million or more; their income from those assets may be relatively modest. For example, an independent store owner could have a large inventory that took years to build up by reinvesting profits back into the business. For another example, an independent farmer could own a couple hundred acres of valuable land that was likely passed down through generations. Both of these small business owners could be struggling to make a living; they are far from wealthy. When these small business owners die, liberals would want to impose a hefty tax on the value of their estates. The result is that their heirs, who very well may not be at all wealthy, must either come up with a lot of cash or must sell the assets (the store or the land). Thus businesses are closed, small farms are swallowed up by large corporations, and jobs are lost.

The liberals' constant insistence that the wealthy should pay more taxes is misguided, misleading, and often destructive. The wealthy, as defined by liberal policy, are often not wealthy at all, just regular people trying to make a living and taking risks doing so.

Aside from the small businessperson, consider an ordinary middle-income couple who worked hard all their lives, saved money, invested wisely, bought a home, paid off the mortgage, and finally retired. The fruit of their half-century of labor and wisdom is an estate worth perhaps $3 million, including their home, possessions, and investments. Assume the couple wanted to leave their estate to be divided among their three children and seven grandchildren. That's a modest $300,000 per heir.

If the liberal Democrats succeed in letting the Bush tax cuts expire, thus reinstating the estate taxes, this family would effectively have to pay $1,100,000 in taxes on that estate. The formula is complicated, but the bottom line is effectively a tax of 55 percent on anything above the first $1 million. The result is the inheritance for each heir in the above scenario would be cut by $110,000. This is another case where the liberals' taxing only the wealthy is hardly that.

This tax money taken by the government from working Americans would then go into the government treasury. It would help fund government programs, including paying for services to illegal immigrants, paying for people to stay home and have babies, paying for college loans that were not repaid, paying to bail out businesses that engaged in bad practices, and so on. It would also help pay for the large congressional staffs and other government waste.

Consider another scenario based on a real-life situation I heard about recently. A very successful company, owned by a husband and wife, is worth approximately $50 million. Much of the value of the company is in high tech assets used in their production processes and systems. The company employs approximately one thousand workers in several plants.

The owners are aging and wish to pass on the business to their four children. Their concern is, if the Democrats succeed in reinstating the inheritance tax, they will not be able to. The children do not have the $27 million that would be owed in tax under the Democrats' plan. They would be forced to sell the business to pay the tax. Furthermore, they would be forced to sell in a tough market and probably could not get full value.

Anticipating this possibility, the family has succeeded in finding a prospective buyer who is willing to pay the $50 million. The buyer has determined that he cannot make a satisfactory return on that investment if he keeps production in the United States. He intends to sell the plants in the United States and set up production in Asia, where labor costs are much lower. The result is the loss of a thousand jobs in the United States. This is another example of how the tax-and-spend policies of the progressive liberal Left destroy the economy and shift job overseas.

The progressive liberal argument against capitalism is similar to the positions of Communists like Stalin and Lenin. They used that argument to rally the populace against capitalism and sell them on their vision of a state-run economy. Anyone with the simplest of historical knowledge understands the misery and abject failure of communism (and socialism) as an economic and political system.

Business is the engine that has made our economy the world's best. It makes sense to fuel the engine with policies that favor enhancing, not restricting, the opportunity to make money and grow.

The government does not produce any goods or create any jobs that produce goods. The government can only tax, pass laws, and spend. Jobs that produce goods and services are created in the private sector. There is nothing that increasing taxes on business can do that will result in more jobs (other than government jobs) or more creativity.

8

- - - - - - - - - -

Republicans Aren't So Great Either

For too long, mainstream America has reacted passively to the encroachment of liberal progressivism. With each new loss of our liberties and redistribution of our tax dollars, too many conservatives have simply shaken their heads, griped about it, and let it happen. We can no longer afford to sit on our hands and tolerate those who wish to transform our country into something very undesirable.

Negligence and irresponsibility by Republicans has allowed the progressive liberal minority faction to take control of the federal government. Many Republican politicians ignore the wishes of their constituents and resort to bad behavior far too often. Conservative Americans have sent many Republicans to Congress only to have them fail to act much differently from the Democrats.

The performance of Republicans in Congress has been shameful. They have demonstrated ineffective leadership and a lack of integrity. Republicans have been weak in standing for true conservative principles and too willing to reach across the aisle to compromise with the progressive liberals. The effect has been moving the entire Congress to the Left and away from basic conservative values expressed by our founding fathers. The concept of reaching across has meant caving in to more and more secular progressive liberalism. The movement to the Left is one reason the progressive assault on our country grows and gains momentum.

As discussed earlier, in 1994 the Republicans took control of the House for the first time in forty years. The Republican Congress crafted its "Contract with America," a pledge to reverse the government spending and expansion of Clinton's first two years. They managed to get ten spending-reduction bills through the House, only to have most of them shot down by the still-Democrat Senate.

The sad irony is that the Republicans finally gained control of the Senate, along with the House and a Republican president, and proceeded to ignore the precepts of the earlier Contract. Spending for practically everything addressed in those ten earlier bills increased under Republican leadership, leading to their control being terminated by voters in 2006 and 2008.

When Republicans lose seats in Congress, it is not because the nation wants more of what the Democrats have to offer. It is because Republicans do not act like the conservatives they said they were. It is because they engage in the same politics as liberals. Republican politicians are just as guilty as their Democrat counterparts of engaging in vote-selling and earmark spending. They are all guilty of allowing corrupt big business practices. Moderate voters considered the actions of previous Republican majorities as corrupt and irresponsible, so they dropped their support. Conservatives and moderates expect a higher standard from their representatives.

My guess is that the secular progressive liberal Left comprises no more than 20 percent of the population. These are the people who truly believe in heavy state control of everything, including the means of production (business) and how everyone's money should be allocated.

There is possibly 25 percent of the population that is relatively uneducated and pays no income taxes. They prefer the Nanny State and believe that liberal Democrats are looking out for them. Frankly, the only reason that Democrats do not win every national election is that this group of people doesn't vote in heavy numbers.

There is another 15 percent or so of the population that can be called "Blue Dog" or "Yellow Dog" Democrats. These are the moderates discussed earlier who vote Democrat in spite of their basic conservatism. Many of them just don't like and don't trust Republicans. Often, I don't blame them.

Assuming a weak turnout of the poor and uninformed, I conclude that there are approximately 35 percent of voters who always vote Democrat. Close to 40 percent of voters always vote Republican or for a Libertarian candidate. That leaves a group of swing voters, the other 25 percent, who decide elections. Given that at least half of the eligible population does not bother to vote, the group of independent swing voters is only 10 to 12 percent of the population. My opinion is that most of those swing voters are ideologically fairly conservative. However, those voters will not tolerate political bad behavior and will not support Republicans who do not meet their requirements.

We saw how voters reacted in the 2006 congressional election. Given control of the House, the Senate, and the presidency in 2002, Republicans spent the next four years failing to execute the will of the voters who elected them. They spent too much money and failed to address issues important to their constituents. The major issues of the day were the war in Iraq, illegal immigration, and the federal budget deficit. The Republican leadership did little to convince the American people they were in control of anything. They failed to control spending and failed to deliver any meaningful reform. As a result, moderate swing voters turned away from them. The failure of Republicans to stand for conservative principles always eventually results in their losing power.

Conservatives tend to believe that doing nothing is better than doing something questionable. Liberals tend to believe that doing something, even if it's questionable, is better than doing nothing. The result is that Republicans appear to be the "Party of No," while the Democrats appear to be the "Agents for Change." The majority of swing voters view the status quo as bad. Many of them believe that Republicans in power support the status quo.

Why do so many Republican lawmakers, who got elected by promising conservatism, drop the fight against progressivism? Part of the answer lies in their perception of what it takes to remain in office. Too many Republicans realize that their conservative constituents will continue to vote for them because the alternative (voting for a progressive liberal) is far worse. With the confidence of continued votes from conservatives, many Republican politicians act as though they only have to minimize antagonizing liberals in order to keep their seat. What they should honor is the mandate of the conservatives who elected them to fight hard against liberalism.

Too many politicians are afraid to stand for what is right for fear of offending a group of people. Many minority people are easily offended, sometimes without real cause. Too often, politicians do the wrong thing for fear of being accused of being racist, homophobic, sexist, or uncaring. Far too many politicians are less interested in doing what's right for their constituents than doing what will get 50.1 percent of the vote in the next election.

As pointed out earlier, the only time in the past fifty years that Republicans enjoyed the majorities in both the House and Senate and a Republican president was the two consecutive terms from 2003 to 2007. Conservatives were ecstatic with the sweeping takeover of Congress in the November 2002 elections and all the opportunity that engendered for taking the country in a great direction. President Bush enjoyed an extremely high approval rating because the economy was robust and because of his national security leadership. Internationally, we enjoyed great respect and a tremendous leadership position, demonstrated notably in November 2002 by the United Nations Security Council voting unanimously (15-0) in favor of the United States' intentions regarding Iraq.

What happened over the next four years should stand as a great example of power squandered and then lost. It should serve as a severe warning to Republican politicians of what can happen when you take what voters have given you and do not use it as promised and as expected.

We expected decisive destruction of the Taliban, al-Queda, and terrorism in general. Instead, we pursued a poorly developed strategy of less than full involvement, waging war "on the cheap" rather than using overwhelming combat power. Volumes have been written about how overwhelming combat power is the only decisive action; partial commitment is rarely effective. President Bush ordered a change in that strategy (the Surge) that led to eventual victory in, and withdrawal from, Iraq. However, that was too late to help the Republicans at the polls in 2006.

We expected a stop to the progressive growth of the federal government. Instead, Republicans did not promote the necessary measures to reduce the size of the government. Instead of acting like fiscally responsible conservatives, they passed liberal spending bills, which Bush continued to sign, bills that conservative voters would have wanted vetoed. Other than his veto of the Stem Cell Research Enactment Act in 2006, Bush did not veto a single spending bill until after Democrats gained control of Congress.

We expected the government to enforce our immigration laws. President Bush supported immigration reform, but it did not happen, so that problem continues to worsen from the terrible state it was in already. We expected the government to stop spending our hard-earned tax dollars for social and health services to people who are in this country illegally, but instead, that grievous form of welfare continues.

We expected our leaders to monitor economic trends and curtail spending practices that could damage the economy. We never expected Congress to continue to support irresponsible lending practices, which resulted in the housing and banking disaster. We expected control over practices that allowed executives of failed companies to walk away with obscene severance or retirement packages.

We expected improvement in our energy policy that would lessen dependence on foreign oil. We expected changes in environmental policy that would make sense. We got neither.

We expected real health care reform, including tax deductions for individuals, pooling for small businesses and individuals, shopping across state lines, insurance not based on employment, limits on malpractice awards, and serious tort reform. We got none of that. Instead, in December 2009, Congress and President Obama chose to reinvent the nation's health care system by legislating a federal government takeover.

In most of these cases, it seems the majority was denied its wishes by the minority. Have we become a nation that is so afraid of offending someone that we will not do what is best for the majority and for the country's well-being?

In fairness, George Bush should get credit for trying to introduce some of the reforms that most of us wanted, but he got nowhere. As mentioned earlier, this was because of the following:

- The utterly unprofessional, irresponsible, and biased media criticized, hounded, ridiculed, and undermined the presidency with its unabashedly inaccurate portrayal of information. Those who get their information from the likes of *Time* magazine, the *New York Times*, CNN, MSNBC, CBS, NBC, ABC, "The View," various talk show hosts, college professors, and Hollywood bought into the Left's hate campaign toward Bush. Their profoundly dishonest and nonobjective news reporting helped cause the next two points.

- Republican politicians did not effectively fight for real conservative values. Many of them stood aside and let the economy deteriorate. Perhaps they thought outspoken support for conservative principles would hurt them politically. Well, some of them found out in 2006 and 2008 the folly of that position.

- Once they regained the majority in Congress, Democrat politicians, emboldened by their media allies, seized the opportunity to stonewall the Bush administration, all the while blaming Bush for everything imaginable.

Republicans have not stood for their principles as aggressively as Democrats. If there is one thing that most Democrat politicians have that eludes many Republican politicians, it is passion. Without passion and emotion, a Republican looks like an accountant in a debate with a charismatic orator. It should be obvious which style most voters respond to.

Conservatives in this country want impassioned conservative leadership. We don't usually get it. We got it from Reagan and to a lesser extent from the Bushes, but we don't get nearly as much of it from our congresspersons as the other side gets from its.

Maybe that is because liberals care less for facts than conservatives, and it's easier to be emotional and eloquent when the truth is irrelevant. After all, simple logic and the truth are often a lot less exciting than fantasy.

We know what happened in 2006 when the Republicans squandered their leadership opportunity. Voters replaced Republicans with progressive liberal Democrats in Congress by the dozens. That event should wake up all Republican politicians. We conservatives want our legislators to lead according to the Constitution and with fiscal responsibility. We do not want them to follow the lead of those would tax and spend, increase the size of government, disregard the Constitution, and destroy our values.

Another failure of Republicans is reflected in the installment of more and more progressive court justices. At the district and appellate levels, we have many judges who are extremely liberal and rule according to opinion, often disregarding the Constitution or the will of the people. Republicans in Congress have not fought as diligently to bar liberal judges as the Left has fought to block conservative ones. One of the reasons for the movement of the federal courts to the Left is because Senate confirmation is required for their installment. As we have noted, Democrats had the majority in the Senate for fifty-six of the past seventy-eight years. Therefore, it has been harder to obtain confirmation for a conservative than for a liberal.

In an effort to attain confirmation, Republicans have nominated many moderates who ultimately moved to the Left. In the case of the Supreme Court, Eisenhower appointed Brennan, who became a liberal. Ford appointed Stevens, who became a radical liberal. Reagan appointed O'Connor, who became a swing voter who often sided with the liberal position. George H. W. Bush appointed Souter, who became a liberal.

Meanwhile, many Republicans have been soft on opposing the liberal justices appointed by the Democrats. The result is that we have courts that often minimize the United States Constitution as the basis of the laws of the land and the rights of American citizens.

Many of us realize that the progressive policies of the extreme Left are destructive and often unconstitutional. We know we must fashion a significant course of corrective action for many policies that have spread like cancer. We cannot just say no to legislation proposed by the Left. We must take aggressive corrective action. Those of us opposed to progressivism and liberalism must push for legislative reform that accomplishes the ideals in which we believe.

We must elect representatives who truly want to do what is best for the American people. We must learn to keep legislators who support the legislation we want and dismiss those who don't. We must do more homework on our politicians and be vigilant about holding them to our standards. We cannot cast a ballot for someone based on appearances, oratory skills, and promises, as most on the Left do. We must know what our representatives are supporting and act accordingly.

Too many citizens cannot name their congressional representatives. The Internet makes it easy to stay informed about your representatives. Type in a search box "US representatives from [your state]" or "US senators" to find out who your representatives are. Type in a search box "Senate [or House] vote on health care" (or any other topic) and find out how your people voted. It's easy to do and it's also easy to use the Internet to let your representatives know what you're thinking. Simply go to their websites, find the "Contact Me" option, and send them a message.

The extremely uninformed and many on the far Left will not do what I'm exhorting you to do. Most of them will continue to vote based on feelings instead of logic, on idealism instead of practicality, on political correctness instead of common sense, and, as always, based on their hatred for the conservative Right and their utter disregard for the Constitution and for American culture and tradition.

We must do better than that. If we want to act on facts instead of fiction and on conservative values rather than progressive liberalism, we must know what we're doing. Don't take for granted that something that sounds good is true. Understand the consequences of proposed legislation. Tell your senators and your representative what you want. Make them squirm the next time they consider voting for more spending or another liberal policy.

A lot of conservatives and libertarians are justifiably fed up with Republican politicians. Now, however, is not the time to split the Republican party and thus hand seats to the Left. That most notably happened when well-meaning conservatives voted for Ross Perot, thus electing Bill Clinton.

At this critical time in our history, it is imperative that conservatives stand united against the progressive assault and vote as many progressive liberals out of office as possible. Our first priority has to be to get rid of the progressive liberals and socialists on the Left. The second priority is to replace Republicans who do not represent conservatives with those who will.

Of course, there are moderate Democrat congresspersons who have the best interests of their constituency in mind and who support the Constitution. Unfortunately, we still see those moderate Democrats caucusing with and voting with the progressive liberal far Left. The political system, with career politicians, makes it extremely difficult to vote against the liberal agenda pushed by the majority of the party. Thus the "I vote for the person, not the party" position very often results in quite the opposite.

When the Republicans regain the majority in the House of Representatives and the Senate, their mandate will be to learn from the failures of the last Republican-majority Congress and act in the interests of the constituency that gave them the power. If they do not, they deserve to be voted out. With heightened awareness and participation among conservative voters, I doubt that Republican legislators will be able to ignore the will of their constituents and keep their offices as easily as they have in the past. That is one of the significant contributions of the Tea Party revolution.

The majority of Americans are not progressive liberals, so why should we have to live with progressive liberal policies? If enough independent voters are convinced that voting with the Left is not in their best interests, we can take control of this country away from those who would transform it into something we don't want. We can reclaim our individual liberties as provided for in the United States Constitution. To do so requires that we vote the progressive liberals out of office. It also requires that the conservatives who replace them act in the interests of their constituents.

Not every incumbent is a crook who needs to be voted out. There are some good conservative constitutionalist legislators— too few, but there are some. We can identify the good lawmakers and identify the bad ones; we must keep the good ones and replace the bad ones.

9

The Third Great Islamic Jihad

We are in a deadly struggle to preserve our country, the Western world, our freedoms, our economy, and our lives from destruction by a very large group of fundamentalist Muslims. Inspired by their Qur'an and the belligerent and violent teaching of their leaders, they are as much (or more) of a threat to modern culture as any group in history. Their stated, written, and demonstrated objective is to convert, subjugate, or destroy Western civilization. The menace of Nazi Germany and Imperialistic Japan during World War II and the threat of the Communist Soviet Union that followed were not as sinister as that of fundamentalist Islam.

Many followers of Islam and Muslim sympathizers will be offended by this assessment. I do not practice the sort of political correctness that supports the spread of extreme fundamentalist Islamic beliefs. If you are a follower of Islam, you should consider why many non-Muslims don't understand how your religion could produce so many murdering savages. Christians and Catholics committed horrible atrocities in the name of religion in other periods in history, but those were long ago, in far less civilized times. It has been many years since mass murder was committed by Catholics or Christians in the name of religion.

Please spare us the Timothy McVeigh argument. McVeigh did not blow up the federal building in Oklahoma City in the name of Christianity, and he was not part of a large group of murderers. He was an anti-government idiot with one accomplice.

Islam is the second most popular religion in the world, with over 1.5 billion followers. Christian, Catholicism, and Jewish religions total roughly 2.1 billion. Interestingly, the third most popular religion is non-religion, including atheists, agnostics, and other secular nonbelievers.

Charles Krauthammer, the eminent commentator and columnist for the *Washington Post*, in discussing the Ground Zero mosque proposal in his August 20, 2010 column, wrote the following:

> Radical Islam is not, by any means, the majority of Islam. But, with its financiers, clerics, propagandists, trainers, leaders, operatives, and sympathizers-according to a conservative estimate, it commands the allegiance of 7 percent of Muslims, i.e., more than 80 million souls-it is a very powerful strain within Islam.

Consider that for a moment: 80 million people who believe in the savage law of Sharia, that all non-Muslims must be converted, subjugated, or killed. That's 80 million people in this world who condone the rape, murder, mutilation, or torture of you, your spouse, and your children!

Note that Krauthammer's estimate suggests only one in fourteen Muslims is a fundamental supporter of jihad, so he asserts the great majority of Muslims are not militant murderers. Also note, however, that practically all terrorist acts being committed in this century are by Muslim extremists.

In case a reader discards the above estimate as exaggerated, assume that estimate is completely out of hand, that the real number is only 10 percent of the number Krauthammer suggests. That is still 8 million militants, more than triple the number of United States military and reserve personnel. Consider also that many so-called peaceful Muslims allow their children to be taught Islam by the clerics, many of whom have consistently demonstrated their militancy. We cannot assume that the children of tolerant Muslims will likewise be tolerant of non-Muslims. There is a very aggressive objective among many fundamentalists to teach jihad to new generations.

During President Obama's 2009 "Apology Tour," he stated that "America is not—and never will be—at war with Islam." That is the position that nearly all Americans would prefer. We do not want war. We do not seek war. We only go to war to protect ourselves, to protect allies, or to protect innocent peoples.

However, Obama's assessment is idealistic, naïve, and dangerous. Fundamentalist Muslims consider themselves at war with America. They don't consider themselves at war with only certain people within America; they are at war with all of us. For that matter, they are at war with everyone who is not one of them, including other Muslims. Consider the Muslim concept of the "Third Jihad," one stated objective of which is the imposition of Islamic rule in America. Terrorism and jihad are intrinsic parts of fundamental Islam.

There is no other major religion in the world that advocates murder of nonbelievers. Like Islam, other religions preach conversion of nonbelievers, but unlike Islam, other religions do not preach enslavement of, or destruction of, those who do not convert. Clearly, fundamental Islam is a religion that condones hate and violence, hardly love and peace, toward non-adherents.

Nations dominated by Islam are the only significant theocracies still in existence. Theocracy is a form of government in which a god or deity is recognized as the state's supreme civil ruler. Generally, a civil leader is believed to have a direct personal connection with God. In the case of Islam, the original civil leader was Muhammad. Practically all other governments are secular in nature, despite the influence of a particular religion. The distinction is that Islamic nations follow the law taken from a single religious source, the Qur'an.

It is not just Christianity and Judaism with which extremist Islam considers itself at war. Islam is intolerant of all other religions. Consider the animosity that exists between Muslims and Hindus in India and Pakistan. Consider that Muslims can't get along with Buddhists either. *It appears that Muslims have no tolerance for anyone else.*

A highly motivated opponent is a deadly opponent. We are not as dedicated to killing them as they are us, mostly because we are civilized and they are savages. They are motivated; that much is obvious from the zeal they have demonstrated time and again. They are willing to kill themselves to kill us, even sacrificing their children as suicide terrorists.

The encroaching and escalating actions of fundamental Muslim terrorists against the United States and other civilized nations is obvious. From the time of the Munich Olympics hostage taking in 1972, the litany of murderous actions by Muslims against innocent people has been staggering, including the following:

- The Iranian revolution by Muslims that included taking American hostages in 1979 (fifty-three Americans held hostage for over 400 days).

- The 1983 bombings of the US Embassy in Beirut (sixty-three killed) and the Beirut Marine barracks (244 US Marines killed, plus fifty-eight French troops killed in a simultaneous attack).

- The restaurant bombing in Spain in 1985 (eighteen US servicemen killed).

- The first World Trade Center bombing in 1993 (six people killed, more than one hundred injured).

- The Khyber Towers bombing in Saudi Arabia in 1996 (nineteen American servicemen killed and over 500 persons wounded).

- The US Embassy bombings in Nairobi, Kenya, in 1998, killing twelve US citizens and wounding over 5,000 people.

- The bombing of a United States warship, the USS *Cole*, in Yemen in 2000 (seventeen US sailors killed, thirty-nine injured).

- Numerous murders, assassinations, and other criminal actions during the past three decades.

So, after the failure of the United States to fully appreciate and react to these actions by a motivated and savage group of ideological and cultural enemies, on September 11, 2001, nineteen fundamentalist Islamic terrorists hijacked four United States commercial airliners and murdered 3,025 innocent people.

In 2008, a group of Islamic terrorists conducted a series of coordinated shooting and bombing attacks across Mumbai, India's largest city. At least 175 Indians were killed and more than 300 injured.

In 2009, there were thirteen cases of Islamic terrorist acts perpetrated to kill innocent citizens around the world; eleven of these attacks were unsuccessful, but two were at least partially successful. Obviously, the terrorists know we cannot stop them all, so they keep vigorously trying.

Since September 11, 2001, there have been over one hundred and twenty acts of violent terrorism attempted by terrorist Muslims. Most of them were thwarted. Many of them were stopped before they unfolded by the intelligence gathering activities of various agencies, notably the Federal Bureau of Investigation. The most effective means of uncovering planned terrorist actions has been the use of informants cultivated by the FBI and other agencies.

Consider that a council of supposed moderate, peaceful Muslims condemned the use of informants by the FBI. How can we tell which Muslims with whom we are at war if the Muslims who say they don't want to be at war refuse to identify themselves and join the battle against those who do?

It makes no sense to continue politically correct practices that endanger American citizens. We should search for terrorists, not search for weapons. Terrorists kill people; weapons are merely tools. We might stop 99 percent of the weapons that go through our airports, but that doesn't mean we are stopping terrorists themselves.

We know the profile that most closely fits those who would kill us. It is absurd not to act on that. The Israelis do, and no one comes close to hijacking an Israeli airplane. We should provide additional security screening for anyone who fits that profile. It is far less a violation of someone's individual rights than it is a protection of the rights of the population.

It makes no sense to hamper our intelligence gathering capability in this time of greatest need to uncover potential threats.

It is irresponsible and dangerous to soften our interrogation techniques and restrict our wire-tapping of cell phone calls coming from known terrorist hangouts. Because of those intelligence gathering techniques, we have uncovered and prevented a number of potentially devastating terrorist plots.

Closing the prisoner of war facility at Guantanamo Bay is another example of a politically motivated strategy that ignores the nature of the threat. Moving the prisoners held there to US soil and bringing them to trial in civilian courts is more than irresponsible. Granting them Constitutional rights meant only for United States citizens is completely misguided and insulting to American citizens. It is absurd to maintain that enemies of our citizenry deserve rights meant for our citizens.

We captured the savage who masterminded the 9/11 attack. In my opinion, it is more than appropriate to strap him to a table and hook up some electricity to sensitive body parts while asking him questions that could result in saving American lives. It is the right course of action to protect our country. The United States demonstrated its civility by subjecting him only to waterboarding, a technique that may be horribly frightening to undergo but causes no permanent physical damage. We have idiots in our midst who would decry the use of this technique as inhumane and who would show even more idiocy by advocating trying this mass murderer in United States criminal court.

Alert passengers and crew on a United States commercial aircraft stopped the Christmas Day underwear bomber from committing mass murder. Why on earth would we suspend interrogation of this animal in order to treat his (non-life threatening) wounds and read him the Miranda rights of US citizens?

When has a country ever given captured enemy combatants the humane treatment and special rights that we are giving these terrorists? Did we bring Nazi or Japanese war criminals to New York City and try them in civilian criminal court?

The enemy we are fighting, fundamental Islamic terrorists, does not adhere to any moral code of conduct, such as the Geneva Convention. They are savage murderers who do not wear uniforms and hide in mosques and in civilian communities. They send women and children on suicide missions and torture and murder Westerners that they capture. They savagely hacked off the heads of American journalist Daniel Pearl and American businessman Nick Berg. They filmed the beheadings and broadcast the videos as a demonstration of what they are capable of doing to infidels. All the while, I might add, hiding behind masks like the cowards they are. They were not signatories to the Geneva Convention and do not adhere to its covenants, so they certainly do not deserve the protections provided in it.

Despite the subhuman nature of the evil against which we are in a struggle for survival, there are people in the United States who are more concerned about the rights and fair treatment of those we capture than they are about the rights of Daniel and Nick and their families.

Consider the case of the Navy SEALs who captured the alleged leader of the butchers who murdered several American civilians working in Iraq. The savages mutilated their victims and then hung them from a bridge and set their bodies on fire. In the course of capturing this grotesque murderer, he allegedly got punched in the mouth and suffered a bloody lip. Three Navy SEALs were put on trial for the alleged abuse of a captured enemy. What could possibly be more idiotic and misguided than that? Has our military leadership stooped to such lowness, in the name of political correctness, that they would actually want to prosecute these guys? Thank God, public opinion was so strong that it saved these heroic servicemen from some stupid, misguided, *liberal* crucifixion.

We must win this war against Muslim terrorists. The Muslim world is growing and spreading, increasing its presence in non-Arab countries in Europe, Asia, Africa, and the Americas. Instead of assimilating into the cultures that exist, Muslims insist on maintaining their own culture while demanding rights and privileges even beyond those available to non-Muslim citizens.

Throughout the history of this country, patriots have understood threats to our existence and have acted accordingly. "Accordingly" means to do all that is necessary to neutralize or eliminate a threat. Many of us who are patriots have difficulty accepting the notion that so many liberals can be unconcerned about the problem of Islamic fundamentalists.

The onerous threat of political correctness is very real. It stands in the way of our being able to defend ourselves properly. When we bend over backward to demonstrate our correctness toward Muslims, to the detriment of the rest of our citizenry, we have clearly gone stupid.

We non-Muslims would like to see the peaceful Muslim community denounce the actions of their violent brothers. Rarely do we see a condemnation from the Muslim community of vicious terrorist acts committed by Muslims. We know that terrorists are often able to hide among peaceful Muslims without fear of being ratted out. Why? Are the peaceful Muslims intimidated? Are they passive because they don't care? Are they sympathetic to the cause of the murderers? I am sure all of these reasons exist to some degree. These so-called peaceful Muslims should be treated as co-conspirators.

Part of the answer may be that it is not possible to be a devout Muslim and be tolerant of non-Muslims. Is it possible to be a devout Muslim and a loyal American citizen at the same time? Here is the Oath of Allegiance that is required of all legal immigrants who wish to attain United States citizenship:

I hereby declare, on oath, that I absolutely and entirely renounce and abjure all allegiance and fidelity to any foreign prince, potentate, state, or sovereignty of whom or which I have heretofore been a subject or citizen; that I will support and defend the Constitution and laws of the United States of America against all enemies, foreign and domestic; that I will bear true faith and allegiance to the same; that I will bear arms on behalf of the United States when required by the law; that I will perform noncombatant service in the armed forces of the United States when required by the law; that I will perform work of national importance under civilian direction when required by the law; and that I take this obligation freely, without any mental reservation or purpose of evasion; so help me God.

Is it possible for a devout Muslim to take this oath sincerely?

Consider the words of Faisal Shahzad, the Muslim convicted of the Times Square bombing plot in 2010. Shahzad became a United States citizen in 2009. When asked by the judge at his trial if he had sworn allegiance to the United States, he responded, "I did swear, but I did not mean it." Sharia law does not honor contracts or promises made between Muslims and non-Muslims. Their law permits and encourages them to lie as necessary to advance their agenda. How then can any Islamic adherent be trusted?

Shahzad built a crude bomb, packed it in a Nissan Pathfinder, drove it into Times Square in Manhattan, lit the fuse, and walked away. Fortunately, his device malfunctioned. Upon being sentenced to life in prison, Shahzad warned Americans of more bloodshed. "Brace yourselves, because the war with Islam has just begun," he smirked in court.

How many Muslim believers does Shahzad represent? More than just an isolated few, to be sure.

I have worked and socialized with people of the Muslim faith who seem to be reasonably peaceful. While some of them may be moderate enough in their Muslim beliefs to be able to coexist with non-Muslims, I wonder how tenable the relationship may be in the long term. Consider how the offspring of moderate, peaceful Muslims get religious teachings. The Qur'an includes the practice of proselytizing and calling nonbelievers to convert to Islam. If the offer to convert is refused, the Qur'an calls for a jihad to be initiated against that person. Jihad allows for the subjugation, enslavement, or annihilation of non-converts. Many Muslim clerics continue to preach this dogma to Muslim children, whether the children are from "peaceful" families or not.

The nature of youth is rebellion against authority and dismissal of parental values. As a result, the children of peaceful Muslims may be quite convertible to the more fundamentalist Muslim position that does not believe in peaceful coexistence.

If Islam is to be considered a religion in which Muslims can exist in peace with non-Muslims, there must be a reform movement initiated by the moderate, peaceful Muslims.

There must be a condemnation and purging from their ranks of the violent Muslims among them. I have not yet observed such an inclination from the imams that represent the supposed moderate Muslims.

You may note that I do not refer to our Muslim enemies as being radical Muslims. I refer to them as fundamentalists, jihadists, and terrorists. I am not sure that Muslim believers in jihad and Sharia law are the ones who are radical Muslims. Could it be that it is actually more radical for a Muslim to be accepting of other religions and cultures?

The Ground Zero mosque issue represents a stark example of friction initiated by Muslims. The announcement of that project and resistance to abandon it are yet another test of the will of the American people to protect itself. Common decency, good will, and tolerance demand that a Muslim mosque not be built there. Does Imam Rauf, who defends its construction, consider religious and cultural tolerance a one-way street, the responsibility only of non-Muslims?

The mosque issue is one of many reasons I have doubts that Muslims and non-Muslims can broadly coexist in a peaceful manner that is in accordance with the Constitution of the United States. Thus, I have reservations that a devout Muslim can be a patriotic American citizen.

Perhaps we should recognize that our pathetically weak, self-destructive, and politically correct posture toward Muslims makes it easier for the fundamentalists among them to pursue their stated objectives. The Muslim community in general does not appear to demonstrate sufficient determination to assist us in defending ourselves against those who seek to destroy our culture.

Of course all Muslims are not terrorists. However, practically all terrorist enemies of the West are Muslims. Considering the seriousness of the threat against us, it would be reasonable to adopt a policy of denying entry into the United States of any noncitizen Muslims so long as we are in conflict with Muslims whose intent is to kill Americans. The admission of large Muslim populations in other countries has certainly not been beneficial to peace or the economic welfare of those countries. Significant and tangible economic, societal, and criminal problems have resulted for any country that has permitted aggressive Muslim immigration.

We should take steps to identify any alien, Muslim or otherwise, who is in this country illegally, prosecute that person according to United States law, and deport that person with all haste. In fact, we should deport anyone who is found to associate with jihadists. We should never permit an enemy of our country and our way of life to gain access to our homeland.

We should immediately remove from the United States military any person who maintains ties to, or correspondence with, known anti-Americans, especially radical Muslim clerics. Behavior like that of the jihadist assassin at Fort Hood would not happen in a United States Army that is not so dangerously concerned with political correctness. It is horribly tragic to think that we send our soldiers to fight a group of people while protecting the rights of the same group of people to infiltrate our military.

Sedition is a term that refers to conduct or speech that tends toward insurrection against the established government. The United States has laws that make seditious activity a criminal act. Surely the behavior of some well-known Muslim and Muslim-sympathizing religious leaders easily falls under the definition of seditious and subversive acts. Why don't we enforce our own laws for the self-defense of our citizenry? We have a lot more to gain than to lose in dropping the idiotic Leftist political correctness that undermines our security interests. We should demand allegiance to the Constitution of the United States from all inhabitants of our country, Muslim or otherwise. Why wouldn't we? Because of progressive liberal thinking? If so, then that's a big part of the problem.

In 1942, shortly after our entry into World War II, my father was a National Guardsman attending an Army school for preparation to attend the United States Military Academy at West Point. Despite being a fourth-generation American citizen, he was investigated by the military because of his German ancestry and his interest in the United States Navy war fleet.

He and his mother sometimes corresponded in German, her being fluent and him wanting to keep up his German language skills. My father's interest in the deployment of our big ships—battleships, cruisers, and aircraft carriers-caused him to follow accounts in the news media of the whereabouts of those ships. Following Pearl Harbor, he suspected that there was information about the fleet that had not yet been made public.

During the war, mail to and from military personnel was often censored (opened and checked) before being delivered. The combination of his unusual knowledge of naval operations and his German language correspondence placed him under suspicion of being a German spy. After a rather extensive investigation, during which the military determined the nature of Dad's knowledge and his language skills, he was cleared. Subsequently, he attended West Point, served as an infantry company commander in Korea, had a distinguished career in the Army and later as an educator.

Neither he nor any organization (like the ACLU) resisted or complained about any civil rights violations, prejudices, or other personal invasions on the basis of his being a "German American." Come to think of it, I never heard my father, his mother, or any of his people ever refer to themselves as German Americans. They were just Americans.

Imagine a similar situation in today's progressive environment. Suppose the military suspected that the Fort Hood terrorist had ties to the enemy, based on his associations, his religion, and his ethnicity, which, if I'm not mistaken, they actually did. Why not investigate, which would possibly have saved the lives of many wonderful Americans? The only reason why not is, again, absurd progressive liberal political correctness.

Again, fundamentalist Muslim terrorists represent the most sinister large-scale enemy in our country's history. Previous large-scale enemies, such as the Germans in both world wars, the Japanese, the North Koreans, the Soviets, and the North Vietnamese, fought as soldiers with some degree of honor. There is nothing honorable, enlightened, moral, or civilized about Muslim terrorism. Their actions and their dogma are subhuman, bestial, dishonorable, and unworthy of the status of a peaceful, reasonable religion.

Why should any American trust a Muslim, regardless of nationality, unless that Muslim is willing to adamantly condemn Muslim terrorists and denounce their using the Muslim religion as the basis for their actions? How can a non-Muslim trust a Muslim United States citizen who prefers Sharia law and culture and does not assimilate into American culture?

Does the Qur'an require conversion, subjugation, or annihilation of nonbelievers or does it not? If it does and someone professes belief in it, then that person's position as an enemy of the United States should be clear.

10

Sharia Law and Useful Idiots

"For evil to flourish, all that is needed is for good people to do nothing." Edmund Burke.

I slam is not merely a religion. It is a political and legal system as well. Islamic law does not practice separation of church and state. The goal of hard core Muslim fundamentalists is to replace Western law and culture with that of Islam.

Islamic Sharia law comes from a combination of the Qur'an, other recorded words and actions attributed to the prophet Muhammad, and interpretation by religious leaders. The application of Sharia law is not consistent among all Muslims, depending largely on the interpretation and religious fervor of local leaders.

Sharia law was born in the barbaric times of the seventh century. Many practices accepted or required by Sharia law are considered by other cultures to be uncivilized and intolerable. Consider the following:

- Homosexuality is strictly illicit, and some Islamic countries allow punishment by death for sodomy or homosexual activities.

- A man is permitted up to four wives simultaneously. Women are not afforded the same right.

- A father can choose a husband for his daughter, and a virgin daughter must have her father's permission to marry.

- A Muslim woman must marry a Muslim man.

- Muslim men may marry and be intimate with minor female children.

- An adulterer can be sentenced to death by stoning.

- Conversion of a Muslim to another religion is considered treason and punishable by death.

- Family members are permitted to conduct "honor" killings under certain circumstances.

- Sharia courts of law do not include juries or lawyers, just the plaintiff and defendant, witnesses, and a judge who has sole authority.

- Most testimony is oral, and the testimony of a female witness carries only half the weight of that of a man. Testimony of a non-Muslim witness can be disregarded altogether.

- The punishment for theft can be imprisonment or amputation of hands. A number of criteria must be met to impose amputation, including the testimony of at least four witnesses (who must be male).

- Drinking alcohol is prohibited. Card games and other games of chance where anything is wagered are prohibited.

- A public dress code compels men to be covered from knee to waist and women to be covered everywhere but hands and face.

Obviously, these tenets are at extreme odds with beliefs and practices in modern Western society. Whereas non-Muslim culture has progressed since the seventh century to provide for equal rights and liberties for everyone, culture governed by Sharia law has not. The severity of the clash between these two worlds depends mostly on the level of fanaticism of Muslim leaders. Many Muslims choose to coexist in peace with other cultures. However, fundamentalists among them seek the conversion, subjugation, or annihilation of nonbelievers. They believe their law gives them no choice.

Islam, as practiced under Sharia law, is an ideology of hatred toward nonbelievers. It rejects the singular principle for which America stands, which is liberty. Sharia law mandates the concept of dhimmitude, which is a status given to non-Muslims who wish to submit to Islamic rule rather than suffer the onslaught of jihad. In this status, non-Muslims are allowed to practice their own religion but with subjugating regulations that deny them equality of rights and dignity. Examples are forbidding dhimmis from possessing firearms or from giving testimony against a Muslim, thus rendering them defenseless and extremely vulnerable to abuse and possible execution.

Fundamentalist Muslims include global jihadists who fervently and violently work to restore Sharia law throughout the Islamic world. The ultimate goal of these jihadists is to impose Sharia on the entire human race, using any means necessary.

What does the attitude and actions of the hard core Left in the Western world have in common with that of the hard core Muslim extremists? The answer is that both enable the advancement of Sharia law. Through their illogical interpretation of the United States Constitution, and their disdain for Christian conservatives, the progressive Left justifies restricting the rights of Christians while protecting those of other religions, particularly Islam. The assault on Christianity is astounding, as is the enabling of radical Islam to expand.

The Muslim practices outlined above are directly opposed to the beliefs of secular progressives in the West, so why would Leftists enable the encroachment of Sharia on Western culture? It is ironic that any Western woman, who enjoys the greatest status for her gender in the history of the world, could think it appropriate to accept the existence of Sharia law in her country. What about homosexuals? In Europe, America, and other civilized cultures, they enjoy nearly all of the freedoms and privileges of heterosexuals. They certainly do not under Sharia law.

Both Hitler and Lenin used the assistance of idealistic fools in the United States to undermine the efforts of those who aggressively opposed them. Lenin coined the phrase "useful idiots of the West." I doubt those useful idiots were political or social conservatives.

Similarly, the advancement of the Islamic agenda needs useful idiots to gain and consolidate its foothold in our culture. It has them in the progressive liberal Leftists who, with their distorted notions of individual freedoms and Constitutional rights, along with their disdain for Christianity and their anti-American sentiment, manage to facilitate the insidious encroachment of Sharia.

The framers of the United States Constitution certainly did not intend for it to be used by enemies of our culture to destroy us. That is an important point that is entirely missed or ignored by progressive liberals. The Left, whose sentiment is demonstrated by the positions taken by the ACLU, apparently would rather let our way of life succumb to jihad than stand against it. Make no mistake about the tactic of fundamentalist Muslims to continue to test the will of those in the West to stand against their advancement of Sharia law. Muslims often make use of the protections of the United States Constitution against us for the advancement of Islam. With the help of the progressive liberal Left, many of them well-meaning, we run the risk of failing those tests.

The progressive Left uses the Constitution to protect the rights of Muslims while citing the same Constitution to restrict the rights of Christians.

It is mostly progressive liberals who are okay with the construction of a Muslim mosque adjacent to Ground Zero in New York. The name of the project to build this mosque is the Cordoba Initiative. That name in itself is sinister and should unite all Americans against it. Cordoba, Spain, was a flourishing city one thousand years ago that was overrun by Islamic jihad.

It is mostly progressive liberals in Great Britain who have allowed the establishment of Muslim courts with jurisdiction over Muslim legal disputes and crimes committed among Muslims. Thus Great Britain has ceded its law enforcement and legal system for Muslims to their clerics.

Muslims violently disrupted a military parade in England and demonstrated aggressively against the military in the United States, but there is no outcry of indignation from progressive liberals. Instead, there is tacit approval.

Secular progressives work to protect the freedom of religion of Muslims while suppressing the same rights for Christians and Jews. Even the current president of the United States refuses to recognize the Christian-based National Day of Prayer yet participates in worship with Muslims.

The Left in America and other countries hinder the efforts of the United States military and its allies in the war against Islamic terrorism. It is the Left that would restrict our intelligence gathering activities and grant rights to foreign enemies that should be reserved for our citizens. The Left joins with Muslim imams to denounce the use of informants within mosques by the FBI.

These actions demonstrate the dangerous alliance of the political far Left and fundamentalist Islamism. There is little doubt of the desire among devout Muslims to spread Sharia law into the Western world and ultimately replace the legal systems of Western countries entirely. The progressive liberal Left is assisting them to accomplish that goal. It should be clear that Muslims are more interested in Americans accepting Muslim culture than Muslims accepting American culture. It appears the American and European Left is willing to accommodate that desire.

The Left is far more willing to accept the spread of Islam into Western culture than the Right. What an irony: the *secular* progressive Left is enabling the spread of a political-*religious* culture!

It is a strange alliance of Leftist Westerners, who view tolerance, diversity, and equality as ideals, and Muslims, who make no pretense of their disdain for those ideals.

Make no mistake about it. Muslims are using the American far Left to advance their influence. With each foothold gained with the help of ignorant and idealistic progressives, a new demand surfaces. Muslim fundamentalists continually test and probe the will of Western societies to stand against them. The Ground Zero mosque is an obvious example. Their strategy is to bully America into submission. Give in and the next test will follow.

When we have failed enough tests, enabled by the Left, they will have gained enough power to destroy our culture. When that happens, they will be ruthless. At that point, will the radical Muslims then thank their allies, the American Left, and allow them to share in the blissful coexistence so wished for by the Left? No, they will just force them into subjugation or exterminate them.

It should be obvious that non-Muslim women and homosexuals are imperiled by radical Islam. How about Jews? Haven't they been designated by Islam to convert to Islam or be destroyed? It is the progressive Left that permits the advancement of Islam within our culture. We have only to look at Europe as the blueprint for what may happen in America.

Why would any female or Jewish or gay person not be in mortal fear of the spread of Islam? The great majority of gays and more than half of American women and Jews vote for candidates who support the progressive Left. In so doing, they enable the advancement of Sharia. As discussed elsewhere in this book, we know many citizens do not vote their own best interests because they do not understand or accept the facts. The threat of subjugation by Islam surely is a glaring example.

11

Cut Government Spending

"A government big enough to give you everything you want is big enough to take everything you have." Thomas Jefferson

"Outside of its legitimate functions, government does nothing as well or as economically as the private sector of the economy." Ronald Reagan

Our government has voted to throw the country into massive debt. As discussed earlier, this includes the failure of Republicans to control spending followed by unprecedented out-of-control spending by Democrats. We are hemorrhaging money left and right. It cannot continue. It must be stopped.

Liberals love to portray Republicans as being the "Party of No," insisting that all Republicans ever do is vote No to everything without offering solutions of their own. Considering the size of spending increases sponsored by Democrats, saying No is often a good idea. Doing something is sometimes worse than doing nothing. Politicians should not be measured by how many bills they passed; politicians should be measured on the soundness and validity of what they voted for or against. I would rather vote for a candidate that said No to virtually every increased spending bill than one who voted Yes. Frankly, the country likely would be better off if the 111th Congress led by Pelosi and Reid had stayed home and passed nothing new.

The truth is that the Democrat majority in the 111th Congress shut out Republican participation in much of the process of drafting legislation, not attempting to get bipartisan support for their massive spending bills. In addition, although not widely reported by the mainstream media, the Republicans indeed offered alternative proposals on practically all issues, including health care reform. With their large majority in the House and Senate, the Democrats basically ignored those proposals.

The number of people in this country whose opinion is "the government should take care of me" is enormous. Lawmakers who pander to their votes by supporting destructive policies should get off the low road and have the integrity and honor to eliminate programs that enable bad behavior and bankrupt the country.

This starts with reducing federal spending—reducing the amount of spending, not just reducing the rate of growth of spending. That means cutting back on the majority of government programs. Thinking Americans know that we waste far too much money. We spend billions on government departments that provide little value, and we waste tremendous amounts of money on those programs that do have value. Politicians on both sides of the aisle acknowledge the problem but seem unable or unwilling to do anything about it. We waste vast amounts of money because we have a bureaucratic system that does not work. This wasteful spending of money we don't have leads to borrowing money, including borrowing from foreign entities, such as China.

The amount of United States debt owned by foreign countries is massive and dangerous.

Since the current recession began in 2007, the number of federal government employees has increased. During the same time, the number of jobs in the private sector has decreased, and overall more people are unemployed. The result is three things. One is the size of the federal government is increasing, thus costing more. Another is that the government is taking over more functions from the private sector. The third is that the economy is weaker.

There is currently no incentive by anyone other than taxpayers to reduce spending. The nature of the beast is that government agencies grow. Policy, procedure, and practice all combine to cause government to get bigger. There is virtually no effort to keep the size of government from increasing. With so much momentum behind increasing the size of government and nothing in place to shrink it, it will take a tremendous adjustment in attitude by both politicians and citizens to accomplish what is necessary to save our economy from disaster.

The following actions constitute a good start:

Make the 2001 and 2003 Tax Cuts Permanent

These reductions in the income tax rates, called the Bush tax cuts, were originally set to expire in 2011. The liberal 111th Congress and President Obama campaigned in 2008 to let the tax cuts expire. However, under duress caused by the takeover of majority control in the House in 2011, Obama worked out a compromise with the Republicans to extend the tax cuts for two years. If that had not happened, taxes would have increased for practically everyone who earns enough to pay any taxes at all. In the *Wall Street Journal* article "What Would Happen if the Bush Tax Cuts Expire," July 28, 2010, Brent Arends wrote the following:

> Right now people pay income taxes on a sliding scale from 10 percent up to 35 percent. The old 2000 rates started at 15 percent and went up to 39.6 percent.
>
> Most ordinary people these days are paying a marginal rate of 15 percent or 25 percent. If we let the tax cuts expire, that might rise for many to 28 percent. Based on data supplied by the AICPA [American Institute of Certified Public Accountants] these ordinary folks would take a tax bump of anywhere between a few hundred and several thousand dollars.
>
> For a typical single filer with adjusted gross income of around $40,000 it might be about $400 a year. For someone making around $80,000, it would be about $1,600 a year.
>
> How about married couples filing jointly? They'd get hit with higher tax rates and a lower standard deduction. (The standard deduction was raised in 2001 to give the middle income earners a break.) A couple earning $80,000 a year in adjusted gross income might pay about $2,200 more. A married couple earning $160,000 a year would pay about $5,500 more. If they have children it would be more, as the child tax credit would revert from $1,000 to $500. Ouch!

Some of the bigger headline changes would be to increase the tax on long-term capital gains and on dividends. The top rate of tax on long-term capital gains—meaning any profits on shares or other assets held for more than a year—would rise from 15 percent to 20 percent. On qualified dividends, it would rise from a maximum of 15 percent to your marginal income tax rate.

Under the current system, notes Melissa Labant, in the American Institute of Certified Public Accountants' tax division, those in the lowest tax brackets right now pay no tax on these sources of income at all.

Certainly, the average taxes on the wealthiest Americans would increase more than it would on average earners, but you can see the effect on ordinary income earners in the $40,000–$80,000 range. President Obama's much emphasized campaign promise that no one making less than $125,000 a year will see a tax increase rings a little shallow, to say the least.

There is also the effect of increasing taxes on higher earners that reduces the amount of money they have available to invest, hire, or grow their businesses. Clearly, the effect is less money in the hands of taxpayers, the money being used to pay part of the cost of the massive programs introduced by the very liberal 111th Congress and signed by President Obama.

Add No New Programs

Any current deliberation on proposed new federal programs should be suspended until the other steps outlined herein are accomplished (outside of needs identified for national defense or Homeland Security).

Freeze Disbursement of Unused Stimulus Funds

It has become obvious that the current stimulus package has failed to improve the economy and is, in fact, an impediment to the economy correcting itself through normal cyclical reactions and business investment. Throwing good money after bad is an old adage that is apparently lost on politicians, particularly those on the Left. The assertion that the solution to debt is more spending, particularly when the spending is not funded, is absurd.

Repeal and Replace the Patient Protection and Affordable Care Act

This act, commonly referred to as health care reform or "Obamacare," calls for the government to take over the health care industry. It was constructed under cover in back rooms and behind closed doors, with shady dealings, buyouts, earmarks, and no transparency. How this bill became law represents the most devious and dishonest side of Washington.

This is a great example of how liberals deceive the American people. Liberals say that Republicans would not participate and want to keep health care the way it was. The truth is that Republicans were not invited to participate in many backroom discussions, and the solutions offered by Republicans were roundly ignored. Liberals like to say that the other side has no plan. Well, the plan that the Republicans offered, the plan that liberals say didn't exist, is outlined below, as summarized on the website gop. gov/solutions/healthcare:

- Lowering health care premiums. The GOP plan will lower health care premiums for American families and small businesses, addressing Americans' number-one priority for health care reform.

- Establishing Universal Access Programs to guarantee access to affordable health care for those with pre-existing conditions. The GOP plan creates Universal Access Programs that expand and reform high-risk pools and reinsurance programs to guarantee that all Americans, regardless of pre-existing conditions or past illnesses, have access to affordable care, while lowering costs for all Americans.

- Ending junk lawsuits. The GOP plan would help end costly junk lawsuits and curb defensive medicine by enacting medical liability reforms modeled after the successful state laws of California and Texas.

- Preventing insurers from unjustly canceling a policy. The GOP plan prohibits an insurer from canceling a policy unless a person commits fraud or conceals material facts about a health condition.

- Encouraging small business health plans. The GOP plan gives small businesses the power to pool together and offer health care at lower prices, just as corporations and labor unions do.

- Encouraging innovative state programs. The GOP plan rewards innovation by providing incentive payments to states that reduce premiums and the number of uninsured.

- Allowing Americans to buy insurance across state lines. The GOP plan allows Americans to shop for coverage from coast to coast by allowing Americans living in one state to purchase insurance in another.

- Promoting healthier lifestyles. The GOP plan promotes prevention and wellness by giving employers greater flexibility to financially reward employees who adopt healthier lifestyles.

- Enhancing Health Savings Accounts (HSAs). The GOP plan creates new incentives to save for current and future health care needs by allowing qualified participants to use HSA funds to pay premiums for high deductible health insurance.

According to the same site, the current plan passed by the Democrats and President Obama will cost Americans up to

$5.5 million in job losses, up to $500 *billion* in Medicare cuts (remember what workers paid for through their paychecks their entire careers?), and up to $729.5 *billion* in tax increases. The Republican plan has none of those costs for Americans.

The effect of the costs of the Democrat plan will be devastating to the economy and to the quality of health care. All polling of citizens indicates that the significant majority of people do not want this legislation. This act should be repealed and replaced with a more constructive and sensible plan. Until a new reform bill can be passed, Congress should vote not to fund the provisions of this act.

Stop the American Clean Energy and Security Act

This act, more popularly known as Cap and Trade (or derisively as Cap and Tax), represents a tremendous threat to the American economy. Under the guise of environmental protection, it would dramatically drive up the cost of electricity and other forms of energy. It would also seriously damage the coal industry. This *Wall Street Journal* article ("The Cap and Tax Fiction," June 26, 2009) sums it up:

> The hit to GDP is the real threat in this bill. The whole point of cap and trade is to hike the price of electricity and gas so that Americans will use less. These higher prices will show up not just in electricity bills or at the gas station but in every manufactured good, from food to cars. Consumers will cut back on spending, which in turn will cut back production, which results in fewer jobs created or higher unemployment. Some companies will instead move their operations overseas, with the same result.

This bill, the product of liberal Democrats and President Obama, passed the House on June 26, 2009, by a vote of 219 to 212. Eight of those yes votes were from RINOs (Republicans In Name Only). The other 211 were all Democrats. As of this writing, this legislation has not been brought to a vote in the Senate. Because of its unpopularity among the voting public, Senate liberals did not want to appear to support it during the 2010 election campaign.

The legislation passed in the House has provisions to phase in the restrictions on the energy industry. Phasing allows for sneaking in objectionable legislation little by little, so that the voters don't know what hit them until it is too late. The loss of disposable income for individuals would rise slowly until the full provisions take effect in 2030. It is estimated that by that time, the average loss in disposable income for each household would exceed $1,000 per year.

Like Obamacare, this legislation is a toad presented as though it were a prince. It is still a toad. Those two pieces of legislation are enough to cripple the economy and burden future generations with unmanageable public debt.

Require a Balanced Budget

According to the Zero-Based Budgeting model, all spending has to be justified each year, without regard for what was spent in any previous years. Ideally, each little piece of spending must be justified before it is approved. Something must be wrong with the system, given the continuous growth of government and its many inefficient and wasteful practices.

Any business, household, or individual knows that it is wise and healthy for expenditures not to exceed income. Ideally, an entity is better off when it spends less than it takes in, saving for a rainy day. Why shouldn't it be the same for the federal government? As we've already discussed, big debt is bad. We should demand that Congress pass a balanced budget amendment to ensure the government cannot spend more than it has.

Reform Entitlement Programs

Practically everyone realizes there is a tremendous amount of waste and abuse associated with many of the entitlement programs, such as food stamps, housing assistance, health care, child care, unemployment compensation, and cash welfare. One half of all money spent by the federal government is spent on social programs, including those programs plus Social Security, Medicare, and Medicaid. That percentage is twice what it was forty years ago.

We all know about the abuses inherent in many of the welfare programs. I understand it is possible for a woman to have multiple children, all out of wedlock, without any income of her own, put them up for foster care, and have a relative become the foster parent. The foster parent could receive around $15,000 in welfare payments per year for each child. Have six to seven such children, and we're looking at a nice six-figure income for the family. There could be one father or many fathers, and he or they could even participate in the lives of the children. The trick is for the dads to not marry the moms and to hide from the system, so they aren't asked to support their own children. Throw in some food stamps, Social Security, and health care, and the lifestyle isn't too shabby.

It is possible, in many states, to draw unemployment compensation for years without ever lifting a finger to look for a job. The system does not attempt to force anyone to make an honest effort to find work. The Department of Labor provides resources to find jobs, but the "artist" (what I call someone who "draws" for a living) does not have to use those resources.

These are but a couple of examples showing abuse of social welfare programs. What is intended to be a helping hand to those in need often is just a handout to those unwilling to work and provide for themselves. In addition, many programs promote promiscuity and immorality by rewarding those who conduct themselves in such a manner.

The federal government and the individual states are derelict for not maintaining tighter controls on who receives subsidies and for what reason. Part of the reason for allowing out-of-control welfare abuse could be because the very people administering those programs, at the level that interfaces with the public, are progressive liberal entitlement people themselves. It is a culture that has spread since the FDR era.

The "cradle to grave" entitlement culture needs to be cleaned up. People who receive benefits should be held accountable for their actions, and those actions should not be producing babies and refusing to work. The qualification criteria for benefits must be overhauled.

Stop Forcing "Green" on America

The Green movement is heavy with good intentions and light on practicality. Many of the notions behind it are based on shaky ground, at best. Spending taxpayer money to promote projects that are not economically sound and not supported by the majority is irresponsible.

Take wind power, for example. I drove across the southeastern California desert toward Inyokern Airport a few years ago and was amazed at the thousands of windmills on the hilltops. As I passed close by, I was impressed at the size of them. I wondered how much they cost compared to the energy they provided. Later I read that they are not cost-efficient, providing less benefit than the cost to build, install, and maintain them. One reason is that the infrastructure is not there to efficiently connect them to the existing power grid. Another reason is that they do not provide a steady source of energy; when the wind isn't blowing, they don't produce. Therefore, it is necessary to also maintain the existing conventional power suppliers, meaning dual systems must be maintained.

Many Green initiatives make sense and do not overburden the taxpayer. Recycling and other trash reduction efforts make sense. However, many of the Green initiatives increase costs to the taxpayer through the use of tax dollars as well as driving up prices and infringing upon consumer freedoms. Such programs should be based on sound logic, not on the ill-founded Gore-type mentality.

Stop the Treasury from Issuing More Debt

We are in dangerous water with regard to our massive debt, much of it owned by foreign entities. At any point in time, our debtors could decide not to honor any more from the United States, which would instantly devalue our currency even more. By refusing to issue more debt, we would force the government to reduce spending, and we would send a message to foreign entities that we intend to strengthen the dollar.

Strengthen Oversight of the Budget

Currently, there are two primary offices whose responsibility is to analyze, report on, and make recommendations regarding the federal budget: the Office of Management and Budget (OMB) and the Congressional Budget Office (CBO). Wikipedia.com describes these offices as follows:

> The OMB is a cabinet-level office, reporting to the president. Its primary responsibility is to oversee the preparation of the federal budget. The top six positions

within the OMB are appointed by the president and confirmed by the Senate. The OMB has several hundred career employees who remain, regardless of who is in the White House.

The CBO is a federal agency within the legislative branch. Its purpose is to provide economic data to Congress. Its director is jointly appointed by the Speaker of the House and the president pro tempore of the Senate.

Neither office has the power to control spending. Neither office is charged with helping reduce the size of growth of government, unless so directed. Apparently, the president and Congress can choose to ignore whatever data are presented to them.

My suggestion is to change the charter of the CBO to give it more responsibility for reducing the national debt and requiring a balanced budget. I don't know any way to do this other than to empower a group to evaluate and monitor governmental expenditures (waste) and cause the necessary reductions to happen.

The people who manage the CBO should have specific experience in managing budgets and running businesses. The people I would empower would come primarily from the business sector but could also include representation from academia and the public sector. Primarily, though, the makeup would be business oriented. Imagine someone with the business acumen of a Donald Trump auditing government spending. If you shudder to think what would happen, you are probably a liberal; if you get a little gleeful feeling thinking about it, you are probably a conservative.

Eliminate Agency Functions

Too many agencies have been created because someone in power decided that a problem exists that needs a government solution. As mentioned earlier, there are several US departments that provide benefits that may not justify the billions those departments cost. According to the Office of Management and Budget (from the government website whitehouse.gov), these are the 2011 federal budgets for the following departments:

- Department of Health and Human
  Services $901 billion

- Department of Agriculture $132 billion

- Department of Labor $116 billion

- Department of Education $ 71 billion

- Department of Housing and Urban
  Development $ 47 billion

- Department of Energy $ 31 billion

These budgets include so-called mandatory spending and discretionary spending. I'm not sure how the concept of Zero-Based Budgeting conflicts with the concept of mandatory spending, but I suspect it does.

These are some of the biggest spenders. Many of the activities of these departments were at some time conducted at the state level or were provided by the private sector.

The Oversight Committee mentioned above should conduct and examine cost/benefit analyses just as done in the private sector. What business could possibly survive on its own without doing so? My opinion is that the departments listed above include many programs that are not cost justified or whose administration should be remanded to the individual states. Government programs that provide little actual benefit need to be identified, challenged, and, if justified, eliminated.

Frankly, my opinion is that we should eliminate the entire Department of Education. Its performance, measured by the comparison of American students' education with that of other industrialized countries, is abysmal. Getting rid of this department, along with eliminating teachers' unions and the tenure system, would likely improve the achievements of our students as well as save more than $70 billion per year of the taxpayers' money.

Some would suggest that government staffing should be reduced across the board by an arbitrary percentage. This horizontal cutting does not address the issue of reducing wasteful government. It's like throwing the baby out with the bathwater. Instead, cutting should be done vertically, eliminating entire functions, executives, and staff.

Reduce Congressional Staffs

The size of these bloated entourages exceeds those of the top rock stars. The following statistics about congressional staffs comes from the websites sourcewatch.com and opencongress.org:

Each member of the House of Representatives may hire up to eighteen permanent employees for their congressional and district offices and spend up to an approved annual monetary allowance. The amount of allowance depends on several factors, such as the number of businesses in their districts, cost to travel to and from their district, and other factors. In 2007, the range of allowances was between $1.2 and $1.6 million.

Senators do not have a limit of the size of staff they may employ. Instead, they are limited by an approved annual monetary allowance. In 2007, their range was between $2.5 and $4.1 million.

Congresspersons do not have to spend their entire allowance. It would be an interesting exercise to look into individual spending. For the sake of this analysis, assume each of the 435 representatives spends $1 million and each of 100 senators spends $3 million. That's a total cost to taxpayers of $735 million.

Reduce the Congressional Liaison Staffs of Government Agencies

Not only do taxpayers have to support agencies that waste tremendous amounts of money, they also have to pay for additional personnel who are basically lobbyists to Congress for individual government departments. These jobs should be seriously reduced. Perhaps clamping down on each agency's budget would take care of this.

Eliminate Presidential Czars

"Czar" is a title given to someone whom the president has appointed to some post to examine some issue and make suggestions. There are many critics of this practice, inasmuch as these czars often are at odds with other presidential advisors, are appointed without congressional approval, and sometimes may undermine congressional oversight. The appointment of these czars is a handy way for the president to circumvent the balance of power among the three branches of government. These appointments are de facto cabinet-level appointments, without the Senate approval that is required of cabinet positions. These appointments, without Senate approval, should be considered unconstitutional.

Presidents are free to create a new job for a czar and staff as they see fit. President Obama made more such appointments in his first nine months than any previous president made during his entire term.

Return Power to the States

Each time the government takes one of those big Left turns, it consumes power that once resided with the individual states. The result is a triple whammy: (1) the Constitutional authority granted to individual states is eroded, (2) the federal budget increases, (3) people in parts of the country have something they don't want shoved down their throats by people in Washington.

A Constitutionally obedient Congress should recognize where the federal government has usurped power that rightfully belongs at a lower level. A responsible and conscientious Congress would seek ways to further reduce the size of the federal government by returning that power.

* * * * *

These are just a few suggestions for making a start to restoring fiscal responsibility to the federal government. There are many other ideas that may be just as sound and equally necessary. It should be a primary objective of lawmakers to explore new ideas to reduce government spending, not look for ways to provide welfare or earmarks for their voters.

12

Real Reform

"that this nation, under God, shall have a new birth of freedom—and that government of the people, by the people, for the people, shall not perish from the earth." The last words of the Gettysburg Address, delivered by Abraham Lincoln on November 19, 1863.

President Lincoln (a Republican) made reference in this address to a nation conceived in liberty and a government of, by, and for the people. Neither the framers of the Constitution nor Lincoln conceived of a nation ruled by professional elitist politicians. They intended a government where citizens chose to run for office in order to represent the wishes of their peers. They did not intend a patronizing government that does not listen to the will of the people and passes law after law that the majority does not want. I suspect they certainly did not intend today's legislative practice of vote selling, pork packing, and power grabbing. Perhaps it is time for "a new birth of freedom."

Our political leaders owe it to the country to recognize and act upon the extreme need for reform. It is far overdue for our lawmakers to change the way they do business in Washington and act more like how they were elected to act. This requires more courage and integrity than legislators have been exhibiting. They would have to act based on the will of the people and the best interests of the country rather than based on their own personal interests.

Legislators must remind themselves, and be reminded by us, just exactly who placed them in office. We hired them; we can fire them. That should be the understanding of every politician, and that should be the power wielded by the voter.

The founding fathers had in mind citizen representatives who went to Washington to serve for a limited time and then returned to their homes to resume their private lives and make their own fortunes. The founding fathers never intended for elected officials to make their fortunes from their public office. Today, we have career politicians who, by getting elected once, are able to ride the bias inherent in incumbency to keep being re-elected to one term after another. The current system produces politicians who are more interested in re-election than in public service. The longer they stay in office, the more they become politicians who do not represent the wishes of their constituents.

The prevailing focus in Washington is on keeping power, regardless of what behavior it takes to accomplish that. Keeping one's seat too often requires politicians to base their votes not on the will of the constituency but on that which ensures re-election. It means pandering and selling out. We voters need to get some of that power away from the politicians by holding them more accountable.

Our leaders should do the right thing for the country as public servants. That starts with integrity and unselfishness. We need to remove incentives for lawmakers to have re-election as their number-one priority and supply incentives for serving the country.

What follows are some suggestions for how to re-emphasize the will of the people and restore common sense and American values. Many of these suggestions are for reforming the federal government, but some require action at the state and local levels.

* * * * *

Term Limits

The Twenty-Second Amendment to the United States Constitution states that "No person shall be elected to the office of the president more than twice, and no person who has held the office of president, or acted as president, for more than two years of a term to which some other person was elected president shall be elected to the office of the president more than once."

It makes sense to place similar limits on both houses of Congress. My proposal would be to limit service to twelve consecutive years of combined service in the House and Senate. After twelve years of service, each legislator would not be eligible to run for either the House or the Senate for a period of six years, but they could then run again for another (potential) twelve years.

I would also consider changing the length of the term for the House of Representatives to four years, instead of the current two years. Under the current system, designed to give citizens the ability to decide their representation more often, representatives spend too much time working on the next election campaign. To ensure that the people continue to have the power to make a change in the makeup of the House every two years, representatives' terms would be staggered such that half of the House is up for election every two years.

The benefits of term limits are substantial. One is simply the idea of fresh blood, infusing Congress with eager new energy that is not tied to long-term relationships with lobbyists. Imagine the difference in the attitudes if legislators knew they had a limited time before they had to return to real life. Imagine a politician serving for twelve years and then having to re-earn the confidence of voters to get sent back again. Washington politicians are too much like educators where tenure means everything, not performance, just how long they've been at it. Having a limited time in office would have the effect of diverting energy away for posturing for re-election and toward making decisions for the benefit of the people.

Congress should pass legislation that imposes similar term limits on judicial appointments. It is ludicrous that we appoint judges for life. Doing so means they never again have to answer to the people. It was originally intended that life appointments would relieve judges from the influence of politics. Unfortunately, it hasn't worked out that way. Possibly the most damage previous presidents and the Senate have done to our rights as citizens has been to appoint and confirm judges who rule in utter disregard for the Constitution and the law. Federal judges, including those on the United States Supreme Court, should be limited to a twelve-year appointment. Possibly they might be reappointed, but they certainly should have to undergo congressional approval to qualify for subsequent terms.

Reform Congressional Pensions

The guaranteed retirement money that Congress has lavished on itself is excessive and an insult to the taxpayer. Granted, in order to enter public service, candidates might give up a good job or business or pass up other opportunities, but it should not be the burden of the taxpayer to support them for the rest of their lives. Congresspersons should be part of the same Social Security system as those of us in the private sector. They should also be able to pay into a retirement account, similar to a 401k or a Thrift Savings Plan.

Combined with term limits, this reform would curtail some of the current ability of legislators to become career politicians with benefits that assure them of never having to work again. Again, the founders did not intend for politicians to be supported by taxpayers for the rest of their lives. The benefit of legislators having to leave office and return to the workplace would be substantial.

Reform Congressional Pay Increases and Health Care Plans

Congress should not vote on its own pay increases. Congress rarely abuses this privilege, as evidenced by their voting against a pay increase in 2009 and 2010, and I don't consider them overpaid relative to the importance of their work. However, it is far more equitable to tie their increase to the same index used for Social Security recipients.

It is galling that Congress can take over the private health care industry, in utter disregard for the will of the majority, while exempting themselves from it. Congress should enjoy the same health care opportunities as those in the private sector.

The Lawmaking Process

The current system of writing bills for consideration by Congress is terribly flawed, such that almost no legislation is passed that focuses on a central issue. We have developed a legislative system that prostitutes our legislators. Votes on spending bills are often bought, rather than cast on principle. Most Americans do not know that almost every spending bill includes one or more provisions that provide a benefit to a specific congressperson that has nothing to do with legislation for the people. For example, a congressperson that has exhausted his or her office furnishing budget may add something in a bill that funds new drapes or carpet for the office. We don't hear any lawmakers contest these corrupt practices because most of them are guilty of participating in this abuse.

In order for legislators to get backing for a proposal, they must basically buy other legislators' votes by including in the bill something for their colleagues. These extras are called earmarks (money earmarked for a special project) or pork (money directed to a district or an organization to gain support). In addition, much legislation also contains "riders," which are provisions that have nothing to do with the central issue and probably could not stand on their own merit. This system makes it almost impossible to address an area of need on its own.

The attitude on Capitol Hill is silly, like that on a children's playground: "I'm not playing your way because you won't play my way." The problem, though, is that on Capitol Hill, it's not harmless. Legislators will often refuse to support a bill, even if they believe in it, without getting a little something for themselves (you scratch my back and I'll scratch yours). The end result is a federal budget that is out of control and a national debt that is unmanageable.

Suggestions for reducing this practice include the following:

1. Require that all bills introduced for consideration are limited in size to something manageable, that they address specific purposes, and that the language is only for those specific purposes. Each bill should include an opening statement of purpose that outlines the content of the bill, and the bill must not contain anything outside that purpose. Something manageable means twenty to

forty pages, or 5,000 to 10,000 words, or something along those lines.

2. Require legislation that is concise and that addresses specific issues, rather than colossal volumes of legalese that is not readily comprehended and not actually read by our legislators. Congress should tackle issues in small bites, which would accelerate the process and bring bills to a quick vote. Consider one area of potential health care reform, the idea of shopping across state lines for insurance coverage. A simple ten-page bill could make that happen. Another bill could address an area like tort reform. A simple twenty-page bill could address that need.

3. Today's pork and earmark practices must be eliminated. Anything that is currently considered an earmark should be considered as a separate bill, standing on its own.

4. Every bill should be posted on the Internet and available through print and televised media for a period of seven days before being presented for presidential approval.

5. Every bill should include a signature page that includes an oath, such as "Under penalty of perjury, I testify that I have read and understand the meaning of this proposed legislation. If I approve this legislation, I further testify that the provisions within this legislation are Constitutional." A lawmaker's signature should be required in order for that lawmaker's vote to be counted. The same signature page should be included for the president.

Eliminate Political Action Committees

A Political Action Committee (PAC) is a private group organized to elect candidates or influence the outcome of political issues or legislation. PACs allow unions, corporations, or other groups to make sizeable contributions to political candidates or their parties. The nature of PACs enables vote-selling and corruption.

More than half of the top PAC contributors to politicians are labor unions. The following unions give more than 90 percent of their contributions to Democrats:

- International Brotherhood of Electrical Workers

- National Education Association

- Laborers' Union

- Service Employees International Union

- Carpenters and Joiners Union

- Teamsters Union

- Communications Workers of America

- American Federation of Teachers

- United Auto Workers

- Machinists and Aerospace Workers Union

According to OpenSecrets.org, the top PAC contributor since 1988 has been the American Federation of State, County, and Municipal Workers, which has donated $40 million since 1988. This PAC has given 98 percent of that money to Democrats. There is something really wrong with this picture: government employees lining up virtually unanimously for one political party. Is there any possibility of conflicts of interest or ethical issues here?

Obviously, not every member of these unions is a progressive Democrat; some of them are conservatives, libertarians, independents, or centrists. For those non-Democrats belonging to unions, the disservice done to them by their organization through PACs is obvious. Their money is being used in opposition to their interests and wishes.

Restrict Lobbying by Foreign Countries

More than 140 foreign countries have lobbyists in Washington whose job is to influence policies in their favor. This includes agents from countries who are hardly our friends, some of whom are among the worst human rights violators. According to Dick Morris and Eileen McGann, in their book *Fleeced*, these lobbyists are able to hire former cabinet officials, as well as former senators and representatives, to plead their cases at the highest levels. The voices of these foreign agents, not the American public, are heard, and it shows in our country's policies.

Real Transparency

Remember the campaign promises of Barack Obama? He insisted that congressional debate would not be behind closed doors, but broadcast on C-Span. He promised that all bills would be posted on the White House website for the public to view for at least five days before he would sign them. Well, those were nice campaign promises, but quite the opposite has happened. Backroom dealing, with the majority party shutting out the minority opposition, has been the norm of the 111th Congress.

The voices of both sides, regardless of which party has the majority, must be heard and must be available in print to the public. Anything else smacks of conspiracy and dishonesty. How can we know what our representatives are up to when deals are cut in secret rooms?

Lawmakers on the Job

When people gripe about the "Do Nothing" Congress, they probably don't even realize how true that is. The amount of time that our lawmakers spend doing the work of the people is shockingly little. In 2007, Nancy Pelosi pledged that the House of Representatives would restore the five-day work week for its members. That was just another campaign promise broken. The average number of days representatives show up for work is around eight or nine a month.

Not only that, a workday might last for as little as a few minutes, just long enough to call roll and then break for the day. Another workday might include voting on the naming of a federal building, or commending someone, or congratulating an NCAA lacrosse national championship team. Yet another day might include voting to support a cause or honoring the life of someone who did something good.

That workload becomes particularly burdensome when it's time to run for re-election or, worse, running for president. Every two years, every seat in the House is up for election, so that second year requires a lot of time away campaigning. The same is true for the last year of each senator's term. During 2008, while busy running for president, Senators Obama, Clinton, and McCain hardly showed up for work at all.

We should insist that the schedules and attendance of our lawmakers be posted on the Internet so that voters can see what their elected officials are doing. We need to be vigilant about watching what they do. We need to e-mail them with questions about what they are doing about whatever issues we care about. We need to vote them out when they don't perform to our expectations.

I might comment, however, that as long as Congress continues to pass spending bill after spending bill that forces the country into increasing debt, perhaps we do not want them working more than they do. My suggestion that we hold them more accountable for working assumes that the work they do is beneficial.

Revise the Tax Code

Congress should take the long-needed measure of dramatically fixing the United State Tax Code. The current unwieldy, expensive, unfair, and frustrating set of IRS regulations should be dumped in favor of a simple, fair method of taxation.

One proposal is to replace our current idiotic tax law with a flat tax. Basically, establish a percentage of earnings that goes to support the federal government and apply the same percentage to everyone. While everyone would pay the same rate, obviously the more one made, the more one would pay in taxes. For the benefit of the very low earners, it might make sense to establish a minimum income under which no tax is assessed. Assume the first $30,000 of everyone's income is excluded. Assume the next $10,000 of income is taxed at a flat rate of 10 percent and all income above $40,000 is taxed at the maximum flat rate of 20 percent. The result would be the following:

- An income of $30,000 would owe no income tax.

- An income of $40,000 would owe $1,000 in taxes ($40,000 minus $30,000 = $10,000 times 10 percent).

- An income of $60,000 would owe $5,000 ($10,000 times 10 percent, plus the next $20,000 times 20 percent).

- An income of $100,000 would owe $13,000.

- An income of $1,000,000 would owe $192,000.

With this plan, there are no deductions, no write-offs, no allowances per dependent, and no tax shelters. There would be no separate category for marital status or head of household status. All income is taxed the same and is per-person. There IS no difference in the tax two people pay if they are married or not, and there is no incentive to have children for the sake of getting a tax break.

Most of the "tax the wealthy" crowd would say that rich people aren't paying enough under this plan. That is the same argument they currently use to insist on raising taxes on higher incomes. The counterargument is that this plan gives more incentive to the higher earners to invest and put money back into the economy. The basis for this incentive is that the marginal utility of earning the next dollar is the same as the marginal utility of earning the last dollar.

In any event, the greatest benefit of this plan is primarily that it simplifies taxation so utterly that the overall savings to the taxpayer would be enormous. Imagine no more IRS, which costs upward of $10 billion a year to operate. Imagine the savings to accounting departments in every business or organization. Imagine the reduction of tax litigation. Imagine the elimination of much of the political fighting over taxation.

Another proposal is to adopt a consumption tax, such as the Fair Tax plan proposed by Georgians Neal Boortz (well-known Libertarian author, speaker, and talk show host) and John Linder (retired Republican congressman). This tax is a federal sales tax on spending, rather than the current tax on earning. Under a consumption tax plan, you keep all of your income and only pay taxes when you buy something. Perhaps certain basic items, like groceries, medicine, rent, and utilities, would be excluded from the sales tax. The beauty of this plan is that it puts decisions in the hands of the individual. It also eliminates the IRS and reduces accounting, litigation, and political fighting.

Another idea would be a hybrid of these two plans. Adopt a flat tax to pay for all current and future government expenditures and add a consumption tax that is solely used to pay off the national debt. A flat tax along the lines of that discussed above could support the government. The consumption tax would be a sales tax in the 3–5 percent range that would get us out of debt. The lowest earners would still pay little of either tax.

There are liberals who are proposing a consumption tax, called a Value Added Tax (VAT). However, their proposal is to add the VAT to the current income tax code, not replace the current income tax code. That is what has been done in almost all European countries, and they are currently reaping the disastrous rewards for implementing those taxes.

The current massive tax law benefits lawyers, tax accountants, and politicians. It promotes crime, corruption, and dishonesty. Almost everyone who pays taxes thinks the tax code should be simplified. It is within the power of Congress to do so. Unfortunately, it is not a priority for Congress because it would require compromise that is not likely. The Left likes the higher taxes on the larger incomes provided by the current progressive income tax, whereas conservatives generally favor lower taxes for everyone. A lot of the opposition to tax reform is from those who do not pay taxes. Any wonder?

Most of the proposals to reform our tax structure come from conservatives who recognize the unfairness and corruptness inherent in the current tax code. It is time for the Left to come to the middle on this issue.

Enforce Immigration Laws

The failure of the federal government to enforce its own laws with regard to illegal immigration and its opposition to states that wish to protect themselves from the terrible criminal and economic impact is reprehensible. It smacks of a step in a larger plan to grant amnesty to illegal aliens, something the great majority of citizens do not want. However, many politicians on the Left want amnesty because the majority of Hispanics vote Democrat. That also explains the heinous action of Obama's attorney general in filing suit against Arizona for trying to defend itself from the crime caused by illegal immigration.

Most of us favor some sort of guest worker program that allows for immigrants to follow our laws and legalize themselves. The majority of Americans don't mind immigrants; they don't want illegal ones.

The provision in the Fourteenth Amendment to the Constitution that grants citizenship to anyone born on United States soil should be repealed. This provision was adopted in 1868, just after the War Between the States, to ensure that former slaves would be granted citizenship. That was inarguably the right thing to do at the time, along with abolishing slavery. The provision is no longer needed. We no longer have any former slaves who need this protection. It should be replaced with a provision that grants citizenship to those born of legal citizens. Granting citizenship to the children of those who enter our country illegally rewards illegal behavior and encourages more of it. It is absurd.

In addition, our current law encourages tourists to enter the country for the sole purpose of having a child on United States soil, who will then be an instant citizen. The result is the parents of these anchor babies have the rights to Social Security benefits without having paid a dime into the system. What a great retirement program for these foreign visitors, and what a grievous burden on the American taxpayer!

Speak English

Many historians point out that a bilingual nation is a weak nation, that a society cannot support multiple languages without great difficulty. There are a few examples of relatively stable countries, such as Switzerland and Canada, which have more than one official language. Those countries have supported a multilingual culture for centuries. However, when a large group of people immigrate to a country that has a tradition of only one language and do not learn the language, the result tends to be divisiveness. In the case of the United States, those who do not learn English tend not to assimilate into the American culture.

Our government offers services in both English and Spanish because of progressive liberals. Corporations and businesses do so because they are after anyone's dollar. I wonder how much money is spent in the United States in an effort to cater to Hispanic immigrants, whether legal or not. I understand that greater than 80 percent of American citizens want to make English the official language of the United States, yet our government does not make it so. That should change.

Read the Second Amendment and Read It Again

In another example of ignoring facts that should hit them in the face, many liberal idealists insist it is in society's best interest to increase gun control. Throughout history, abusive and domineering governments have limited private ownership of firearms as a way to minimize resistance to their agenda. It should be obvious that a people without the right of personal protection are a people easily stripped of liberty.

Remember the earlier discussion of the Islamic practice of dhimmitude? Removing the right of non-Muslims to bear arms is an essential part of the subjugation and virtual enslavement included in Sharia law. Would gun control advocates want to subject themselves to the whims of fundamentalist Islamic dictatorial control?

Ironically, when threatened, the gun control crowd flees to the protection of those who will bear arms and use them to defend themselves and others. Whenever the country is threatened, those who stump for stricter gun control measures shrink into the background, only to reappear once they think the coast is clear.

The Multicultural Trap

Many progressive liberals promote the concept of multiculturalism, the concept that people of different cultures should live side-by-side and celebrate each other's differences. This is in direct opposition to the strength of America's culture. The strength of the United States has always been that people come here (other than native Americans, we all descended from immigrants) and become nonhyphenated Americans in the melting pot of unity, not the separateness of multiculturalism.

Angela Merkel, chancellor of Germany, stated in a speech in October 2010 that multiculturalism in Germany has "failed, utterly failed." She noted that Germans and foreign workers who do not adapt to German culture cannot live side-by-side without significant difficulty.

The great majority of Americans agree with welcoming people to our country, to become citizens, to speak English, and to assimilate into the wonderful American culture. That is what the Irish, the Germans, the Italians, and others did in the past. That is what Americans of African descent did as well. For the unique and wonderful American culture to survive, we must require that of all citizens.

The United Nations

Why does the United States continue to participate in and fund an organization that has demonstrated its anti-American bias so overtly? Why does the United States continue to give foreign aid to countries that consistently vote against the interests of the United States in the UN? One reason is because of our dependence on foreign energy sources, like oil from the Middle East. We could change that. Another reason is that we want to be a benevolent nation that wishes to promote global peace and understanding. Frankly, the United Nations is of little value in that exercise.

Most of the rest of the world wants our money and simultaneously wants the right to bash us. I believe that the majority of the citizens of this country would agree that we should tell the UN what we will do and what we will not, rather than vice versa. The UN is a forum for radical enemies like Mahmoud Ahmadinejad and Hugo Chavez to exercise their vitriol toward America. If the United States refused to participate in the UN, the organization would probably collapse (and most Americans would applaud).

Eliminate Teachers' Unions

I read recently that the number of teachers who lose their jobs because of performance is approximately 1 in 2,500. It is absurd to think that 2,499 out of every 2,500 teachers do a good job. Meanwhile, the number of doctors who lose their license because of malpractice is 1 in 47. It is little wonder the quality of education in our country is so pitiful.

There are many wonderful teachers in our public schools. The majority of teachers are undoubtedly dedicated professionals, but there are many whose performance is substandard. Unfortunately, it is nearly impossible to fire or discipline poorly performing teachers. The tenure system makes it difficult to get rid of a teacher who has managed to stay in the job for a while, regardless of ability or performance. In addition, the courts, liberalism, and political correctness conspire to tie the hands of good teachers who would prefer to maintain order in the classroom, demand performance by students, and reward only those students who deserve it.

Teachers' unions, especially the National Education Association and the American Federation of Teachers, block the efforts of school systems to reward good performance. They do not want pay raises based on performance, instead insisting on pay raises for all. As a result, good teachers do not get rewarded, and many of them leave for the better paying jobs in private enterprise, leaving behind the poorer performing teachers.

Meanwhile, these unions sell insurance, investments, and other benefits to members and then skim off hefty fees and percentages, basically ripping off the members. In so many cases, members are shocked to discover that the money they had invested through the union grew far less than the market, not having realized how much the union was taking from them. The actions of many of the leaders of these unions is at best unethical, at worse outright fraudulent.

Our educational system, once one of the best in the world, is now one of the worst among industrialized nations. Remember the discussion of the shockingly ignorant voters in an earlier chapter? It should not be a great revelation, given what is not being taught in our public schools.

Stop All Forms of Discrimination and Labeling

We have laws that prevent discrimination based on race, creed, color, religion, national origin, ancestry, sex, age, or disability.

Unfortunately, often those laws are used to protect only certain groups, those considered minorities. Often those laws are not enforced when the person discriminated against is white, male, or Christian.

There are organizations and groups in this country that base admission on race or gender, in direct contradiction to the intent and spirit of anti-discrimination laws. Often, these organizations are allowed to break the law because of our modern misguided notion of political correctness.

Why is there a Congressional Black Caucus? It is an organization of black congresspersons with the objective of advancing the interests of one race. It has a foundation that provides scholarships, internships, and fellowships for people of only one race. It is an organization whose membership is restricted solely on the basis of race.

In January 2007, Representative Tom Tancredo, R-Colorado, remarked about the existence of the Congressional Black Caucus as well as Congressional Hispanic Caucuses, saying:

> It is utterly hypocritical for Congress to extol the virtues of a colorblind society while officially sanctioning caucuses that are based solely on race. If we are serious about achieving the goal of a colorblind society, Congress should lead by example and end these divisive, race-based caucuses.

There is nothing unlawful about a private organization limiting its membership to whatever groups it wants. I couldn't care less that there is a National Association of Black Scuba Divers (there really is) or The Glass Hammer (an organization for women), but no organization that uses any public funds should be allowed to restrict its membership based on discrimination.

It is time that we realized that the answer to past discriminations is not reversing the discrimination, as the liberal Left so often wants to do. The hypocrisy of standing for equality, while promoting the opposite, is obvious. Not only is such discrimination morally and ethically wrong, it can be extremely dangerous. As already discussed, there is a real threat enabled by the liberal penchant for protecting the rights of Muslims while denying the same to Christians.

Hate crime legislation is another grievous example of progressive liberal inequity. A hate crime is one in which the perpetrator targets a victim based on the victim's membership in a group, such as race, gender, sexual orientation, age, and the like. The intent of hate crime legislation is to impose more severe penalties for crimes classified as involving a motive based on hate.

My question is this: Is a crime committed with a hate motive worse than the same crime committed with another motive? If Jack murders Joe because Joe is a different race and Jack is a racist, is that worse than Jack murdering Joe because Jack is a misanthrope who just doesn't like Joe? Suppose Jack is a nasty bully who beats up a gay kid at school. Is that worse than Jack beating up a straight kid at school? Shouldn't the penalties for these crimes be the same? Motive is a means to help prove a crime was committed. We have penalties for crimes. The penalty should be based on the crime, not the motive.

Here again, with hate crimes, we see the tendency of enforcement in one direction. We don't seem to be as concerned with determining if the motive was based on hate when the victim is not in one of the groups identified as being discriminated against.

* * * * *

There are many other changes that need to take place in Washington and across the country, many of which are money-savers discussed in the previous chapter. Even with the few changes above, we could begin to pare down the complexity and shadiness of what happens in Congress, improve the quality of education, and remove barriers to fairness. Frankly, the improvement in efficiency and effectiveness of Congress that would result from these changes would be very significant. The federal budget process would be greatly improved, and the size of the federal budget would be reduced.

"I pledge allegiance to the flag of the United States of America and to the republic for which it stands, one nation under God, indivisible, with liberty and justice for all."

This is the Pledge of Allegiance that older generations learned in school, memorized, and repeated often. I wonder how many of today's children attending our public schools even know what this pledge is or have ever said it. Anyone who wishes to be a citizen of this country who cannot honestly make this pledge is not deserving of citizenship in the United States and should go elsewhere. I'm afraid that would include a lot of today's secular progressive liberals, as well as most devout Muslims.

13

The Elections of 2010

Much of this book was written during 2010, prior to the November elections. It appears the results of those elections have confirmed what I assert the majority of Americans want. However, I do not like the frequently overused word "mandate." I do not believe it is a mandate when a politician gets the vote of just over half of the people. President Obama's 53 percent of the popular vote in 2008 was no mandate; 47 percent voted against him. By the same token, Republican victories in 2010 do not imply an overwhelming support of conservative ideals.

The elections on November 2, 2010, yielded a Republican majority in the House of Representatives and a reduced Democrat majority in the Senate. The result is that bipartisan support will be required to enact any significant legislation, unlike the case during 2009–2011.

For the previous two years, the Democrats were ruthless and divisive with their partisan leadership. They enacted enormous chunks of legislation that were not popular with the majority of the American people. The reaction of the people was to replace scores of Democrats with Republicans. In addition, the mood of conservative voters was to reject Republicans they deemed too liberal. Clearly, the majority recognized the danger of policies that represented such a hard turn to the Left and voted against it. At the state level, results yielded a significant majority of Republican governorships and legislatures.

The decision of voters in 2010 does not represent Republican support as much as it represents rejection of the policy of the 111th Democrat Congress and the Obama administration. Every decade or two, the country votes to give majority power to the Democrats, which they promptly use to increase the size of government, raise taxes, and promote entitlement.

Here is a synopsis of what the American people accomplished with their votes in November:

- Republicans gained sixty-five seats in the House of Representatives, which created a sizeable majority and removed the extremely liberal Nancy Pelosi as Speaker of the House.

- Republicans gained six seats in the Senate, failing to gain the majority but closing the gap enough to ensure their participation in lawmaking.

- Republicans gained eleven state governorships and hundreds of state offices throughout the country.

- Republicans gained eighteen state legislative bodies while losing none to Democrats.

The very clear message from this election is that mainstream America rejects progressive liberalism. Most Americans are moderate or conservative and support those values discussed earlier: smaller government, lower taxes, strong national defense, and traditional family values. They feel particularly concerned and threatened by the massive debt and expansion of the government advanced by the progressive liberal Democrat Congress.

The message is not pro-Republican. The message is a rejection of progressivism and an emphatic call for moderation and conservatism. Americans also do not want the congressional Republican majority's performance of the recent past, particularly during the Bush years. Reasonable Americans want fiscal responsibility, period.

The message is that Americans do not like having legislation shoved down their throats by those too arrogant to consider their wishes. They do not like massive bills constructed and voted on in the middle of the night, behind closed doors, shutting out the opposition and public opinion. Most Americans know deception, duplicity, and dishonesty when they see it.

The message is that most Americans understand that increasing the size of government with massive new programs requires money that we do not have. Americans realize the negative effect on creating and keeping jobs. Sensible Americans know that the government does not create jobs, other than government jobs paid for by the taxpayers fortunate enough to have a job. Thinking Americans know that the staggering debt incurred by irresponsible spending devalues the dollar, which will ultimately erode savings, retirement, and our economy.

When asked their reaction to the power taken from them in the November elections, several Democrats, including President Obama, commented along the lines of "We did not do enough to create jobs and instill confidence." What is it about the fact that government cannot create jobs that they fail to grasp? Actually, they can create jobs, indirectly, by creating a climate that favors the creation of jobs by private business. As so eloquently stated in our Constitution, one directive of our government is to promote the general welfare, not support the general welfare. Raising taxes and expanding government does not do so.

President Obama and many Democrats just don't seem to get it. They cannot accept or acknowledge that the majority of us don't like their policies. Consider a hypothetical large company that introduced a new line of products two years ago and has seen poor sales results. With all the evidence that this product line is simply not as popular as that of the competition, the Chief Executive Officer (Pelosi), Chief Operating Officer (Reid), and Chairman of the Board (Obama) blithely conclude that their advertising and marketing hasn't been effective enough. Surely the consumers are just not giving the products a chance or are too dense to understand the products. There appears to be an unhealthy mix of delusion, arrogance, and elitism among this company's leadership.

Another example is the decision of the minority Democrats to elect former Speaker Pelosi as House Minority Leader for the 2011–2013 112th Congress. The policies she and the Democrat leadership promoted and forced on an unwilling public led directly to the greatest loss of political power by one party in over seventy-five years. At the national, state, and local levels, the total loss of power by Democrats was many hundreds of legislative seats. She and her cohorts' progressive liberal policies were clearly rejected by the voters.

Speaker Pelosi was obviously a highly effective leader for the Obama and secular progressive agenda. Her effectiveness in getting massive chunks of Leftist legislation passed was remarkable, as was her ability to raise money from wealthy sources. Apparently, her effectiveness was enough to convince the Democrats to put her back in leadership. Never mind the election's clear demonstration that the majority of voters vehemently object to the results of that leadership. This is another obvious demonstration of the power held by the ultra Left within the Democrat party and their refusal to acknowledge the will of the people.

Five weeks after the November elections, Democrats in the Senate presented a 1,924-page Omnibus spending bill to fund the operation of the federal government for the rest of the fiscal year. Citing the urgency of funding the government before the Christmas break, the Democrats intended to get the bill passed without full debate in the Senate and without any scrutiny or input from the people. This massive bill included thousands of earmarks, the very sort of practice the people are screaming they want abolished. As Senator John Cornyn, R-Texas, noted:

> Today we learn Senate Democrats now want to … jam [the spending measures] through in the waning moments of this lame duck session before anyone can read them. This political end-around reveals just how quickly my colleagues across the aisle have already forgotten the voters' message in November.

Another message from the results of the November elections, more subtle perhaps, is that conservatives demonstrated that they vote for candidates on principle, not on race, gender, or ethnic origin. The election of two black Republican congressmen, Allen West from Florida and Tim Scott from South Carolina, demonstrates that message. They are the first black Republican congressmen since J. C. Watts retired in 2003. It is past due for more blacks to be elected as Republicans. It is difficult, but we see it is possible. A black liberal can certainly get elected without the support of conservative white voters, but it is unlikely that a black conservative can get elected without appealing to the white and black conservative community. Conservative white voters are more than willing to support a conservative of a different race. Conservatives also appreciate the courage of convictions it takes for black conservatives to run despite the viciousness they often receive from the Left, the black House and Senate caucuses, and the black community in general.

Putting the lie to the tired old Democrat assertions about Republicans, conservatives clearly demonstrated their attitude toward inclusiveness. In addition to the wins by West and Scott, three new female Republican governors were elected. Susana Martinez of New Mexico became the first Hispanic American female governor, Nikki Haley of South Carolina became the first Indian and Asian American female governor, and Mary Fallin became the first woman to serve as Oklahoma's governor.

The increase in Republican governorships and state legislative bodies is very significant. Not only does it signal more fiscal responsibility for those states, it also sets a different stage for the national elections in 2012. The influence of the leading party at the state level should not be understated. For one, the majority party has more control of redistricting, which can increase the likelihood of its candidates' success. In addition, the majority party has more infrastructure, money, and momentum available to support their candidates in national campaigns.

Consider Ohio, which has voted for the winner in the last thirteen presidential elections and is possibly the state most representative of the makeup and mood of the country as a whole. In the last three presidential elections, the vote in Ohio was very predictive of the national results. Significantly, Ohio had a Republican governor both times Bush was elected and had a Democrat governor when Obama was elected. In 2010, Ohio elected Republican John Kasich over incumbent Democrat Ted Strickland. That shift back to Republicans does not bode well for the Democrat presidential candidate in 2012.

Personally, my biggest disappointments on Election Day 2010 was the failure to take the Senate seats of the ultra progressive liberals Harry Reid of Nevada, Barbara Boxer of California, Barney Frank of Massachusetts, and "Vietnam veteran—not" Dick Blumenthal of Connecticut.

Reid, Boxer, and Frank are all extreme progressive liberals who promote the movement of the country toward socialism. Reid has been a leader in promoting the disastrous spending policies of the Left. Boxer has supported the spending agenda while promoting cultural destruction and opposing national security. She is the arrogant woman who insultingly corrected a United States general for saying "Yes, ma'am," instead of "Yes, Senator." Frank is an aggressive liberal supporter of ACORN and is largely responsible for the disastrous lending practices that devastated the housing and banking industries. Blumenthal is a liberal Democrat as well and insulted our military personnel by lying about his service record.

Californians not only chose Boxer, they also chose to recycle former Governor Jerry Brown. California is a financial and cultural disaster, obviously because of the policies of these progressive liberals, yet the majority of voters continue to support them. California is the eighth largest economy in the world, bigger than that of Russia and Canada, among others. California has amassed a tremendous public debt and is virtually bankrupt. It has no hope of repaying its debt. Yet the voters continue to support one of the most progressively ultra liberal policy agendas in the world. It has a tax structure that basically soaks the so-called rich so it can redistribute wealth to illegal aliens and entitlement programs.

The result of California's tax structure and liberal programs is that the so-called rich and most major business enterprises are leaving the state. This produces a downward spiral with fewer and fewer bill payers. In the not-too-distant future, the state will probably lose nearly all of its sources of income. Regardless of the bleakness of its future, the majority of its citizens continue to support and create more and more indigents. California's economic situation is akin to that of Greece. Who is going to pay California's obligations? Based upon the actions of recent administrations to bail out distressed entities, it appears the United States will not allow California to go into bankruptcy. That means the taxpayers in the other forty-nine states will have to pay for California's financially irresponsible entitlement and socialist programs.

What do the results from 2010 mean for the next two years? That will be determined by the actions on both sides of the aisle. It will be determined by the willingness of the Left to realize that its agenda was rejected by the majority of the people and the willingness of some of them to compromise by moving to the middle. It will be determined by the decisions of the president as he is presented with legislative change that differs from his original agenda. It will be determined by the integrity of the new elected conservatives in carrying out the promises they made to win election.

Many of the Democrats who kept their seats in the House and Senate are among the more liberal, because they represent districts and states that are predominately liberal. Moderate districts and states tended to replace moderate Democrats with conservative Republicans. The result is a smaller group of Democrats that is likely to be more collectively liberal. At the same time, the expanded body of Republicans elected is more conservative as a group than the previous one.

Taking the liberty of categorizing voters into three roughly equal sized groups, the Right, the Middle, and the Left, we can generalize that the following occurred in the 2010 elections:

- The third on the Right who are conservatives rejected Republicans who did not support conservative principles and replaced them with candidates promising to be more to the Right.

- The third in the Middle who are moderates rejected Democrats who supported highly liberal and unpopular legislation like health care, bailouts, stimulus, and other vastly expensive programs and replaced them with Republicans.

- The third on the Left who are committed progressive liberals continued to vote for the same highly liberal Democrats, as usual.

The result is a significant move to the political Right, toward conservatism and moderation and away from liberalism. However, that move does not drag the far Left with it. They are the third of the country that refuses to accept the basic values of the majority of Americans.

I expect the hard Left liberals in Washington will refuse to meet the Republicans in the middle. At the same time, most conservatives do not want the Republicans to compromise on conservative principles, as they have done in the past. That raises the possibility of a stalemate, particularly if Democrats vote as solidly on party lines as they did in the past two years. If, however, a few Democrats realize what the majority of Americans want and vote to support it along with Republicans, conservative legislation could land on the president's desk.

I expect the opening agenda of the Republicans will include addressing the health care package passed by the Democrats. A real battle is almost certainly brewing over this issue. Conservatives and many moderates have adamantly insisted on repeal, in whole or in part, of the health care legislation passed by the Democrats. President Obama may have a hard time admitting that the bill he pushed so hard, his signature legislation, is not only unpopular but destructive. It may be a battle that is fought throughout the two years of this Congress with little satisfaction for anyone.

By claiming leadership of the House, even without the majority in the Senate, Republicans have gained an enviable position. If they hold firm to their promises and conservative values, the Republican-majority House will pass legislation that the majority of people want them to pass. The Democrat-majority Senate may kill it, or the president may veto it, but they will do so at the peril of the mood the public demonstrated in 2010.

That brings us to an analysis of what may happen in the next national elections in 2012. If the Republicans don't completely blow it by abdicating the principles that put them in office, the likelihood is they will increase their majority in the House and win a significant majority in the Senate. Consider the number of seats that Democrats barely held onto in 2010. Consider the number of Senate seats the Democrats narrowly took in 2006 and 2008 as backlash against George Bush and Republicans. All of those are at risk of being lost by the Democrats to the Republicans in 2012.

There are thirty-three Senate seats up for election in 2012. Of those, twenty-four are currently held by Democrats and nine by Republicans. Eight of those nine should remain Republican. The one most contested might be Scott Brown's in Massachusetts. At least half of those twenty-four Democrat seats are likely to fall to the Republican candidate. It is quite conceivable that Republicans could have a veto-proof majority beginning in 2013.

The Democrat party has always paraded its appeal to the young, but their leadership is aging, and there doesn't appear to be young dynamic Democrats looming to take a leadership role. All of the young dynamic types are currently emerging from the Republican ranks. This bodes badly for liberals.

President Obama has a big decision to make. Is he a practical politician, like Bill Clinton, or is he committed to the progressive agenda, far to the Left of the majority, like Jimmy Carter? As discussed earlier, Clinton basically reinvented himself when he lost his majority in Congress, moved to the middle, got credit for the economy's improvement, and was elected to a second term. On the other hand, when the majority objected to Carter's first two years, he refused to budge and was routed by Reagan in his bid for a second term.

In the past, we have seen far too many Republicans fail to hold to their stated values once elected. I believe the unprecedented outrage of the American voter expressed in 2010 signals a change in the rules of the game. My confident hope is that the people will stay engaged and hold the feet of their Republican politicians to the fire. More so than in the past, we see clear evidence that conservative mainstream Americans are more involved, more focused, and more militant. That is what Americans do when threatened.

The voters have given the Republicans another chance, but it comes with serious responsibility. The newly elected Republicans will be expected to practice what they preached while campaigning. Many of the re-elected Republicans are returning to Congress only because they have been viewed as the least objectionable option, not necessarily because of their record. Future support for all of them is contingent upon their honoring campaign promises and acting according to the will of their constituents.

I expect voters on the hard Left to maintain their position. Those on the far Left have their beliefs and will support them regardless. There will always be a significant portion of the country that believes in big government and heavy taxation to support it. There will always be those who favor the One World concept over the traditional American Way. Similarly, voters on the hard Right will contain to maintain their position, thus leaving the future of America in the hands of those moderate voters in the middle.

The voters in the middle expressed their disapproval of the progressive agenda of heavy taxation, out-of-control spending, and politics as usual. They will not support members of the new Congress who do not act with integrity and who fail to do what they were sent to do. I believe moderate and conservative voters will be watching more closely than ever and will not tolerate the politics of the past. It is imperative that moderate and conservative citizens continue to demonstrate their expectations and require elected legislatures to act in the best interests of the country. Our future is at stake.

God bless America.

Acknowledgments

I n writing this book, I sought the advice and wisdom of several people whose opinions I value, including two great friends and former in-laws, Ron Ridenour and Brian Wismer. I engaged a variety of people in conversation, including the owner and patrons of my local barbershop, other businesspersons, employees and retirees, my very wise mother, my stepfather, and many friends and acquaintances. I listened to what they had to say on the matters discussed in this book. Many of those conversations reinforced my belief that I am articulating much of what the majority of Americans think.

The writings and opinions of a number of noted authors, columnists, and commentators helped in forming or supporting my opinions. Among them are (alphabetically) Glenn Beck, Neal Boortz, George W. Bush, Ann Coulter, Ron Ewart, Michael Gallagher, Newt Gingrich, Sean Hannity, Michelle Malkin, Michael Medved, Dick Morris, Oliver North, Bill O'Reilly, Sarah Palin, Dennis Prager, Karl Rove, Michael Reagan, Ronald Reagan, and Thomas Sowell. One may easily note that practically all of the persons mentioned here are prominent conservatives or libertarians. Given the opinions expressed herein, that should be expected.

I have also drawn from the United States Constitution, its amendments, and the Bill of Rights to support assertions regarding the principles upon which the United States was founded and the intent of the patriots who wrote those documents.

I owe a special thanks to my brother Ed, who spent many hours proofreading and making valuable contributions. His many years of service to his country, both as a United States Army officer and in management within the federal government, have given him an informed perspective on politics and American values.

Finally, I would like to humbly and earnestly thank those Americans who make it possible for a citizen like me to express his opinion. They are the United States armed forces men and women who, with great sacrifice, honor, dignity, and skill, preserve our freedoms as well as those of millions of others worldwide. They are also the many American patriots of other professions who work every day to protect the homeland. May God bless them and keep them safe.